The Dog Walker's Startup Guide

The Dog Walker's Startup Guide

Create Your Own Lucrative
Dog Walking Business in 12 Easy Steps

J.D. ANTELL

NOVUS MARKETS

The Dog Walker's Startup Guide
Create Your Own Lucrative Dog Walking Business in 12 Easy Steps

By J.D. Antell

Published by Novus Markets
www.novusmarkets.com

While every attempt has been made to provide accurate and authoritative information the author and publisher assume no responsibility for the information contained in the web sites, books, and other publications, created by others, which are mentioned in this book, nor are they expressly advocating the methods, software, attitudes or opinions contained in them. This book is sold with the understanding that the author and publisher are not engaged in rendering any legal, financial, or other professional service of any kind. Acting upon any of the advice contained in this book or the resources mentioned herein either directly or indirectly is at your own risk, and the author and publisher are not responsible for damages resulting from any action you may take.

Names used by manufacturers and sellers to distinguish their products are claimed to be trademarks and, where known, may be shown in italics. The author and publisher perform no investigation of, and make no warranties or representations regarding, the validity or existence of any trademark right in the names or words used in this book, and no such use should be regarded as affecting the validity of any trademark or other proprietary right. The publisher and author assume no responsibility for errors or omissions with regard to trademarks.

Edited by Marlena Zapf

Cover design by J.D. Antell, photo by Ryan Lane

First Edition

Printed in the United States of America

10 9 8 7 6 5 4

For
Beatrice, my first furry client.
(2002-2008)

CONTENTS

Introduction

Step 1

Projecting Income and Defining Your Business & Services

Step 2

The Business of Dog Walking

Step 3

Creating a Website

Step 4
Advertising Your Business

Step 5
Equipment

Step 6

Client Interview

Step 7

Walking the Dogs

Step 8

Understanding and Minding the Animals in Your Care

Step 9

Earning Trust

Step 10
Troubles You May Encounter

Step 11
Dog Fights

Step 12
Keeping in Touch

INTRODUCTION

Your journey begins

I don't know who or where you are now. You might be a mother contemplating returning to work, an employee trapped inside a dark room (like I was), or someone looking for a supplemental income. In any case, you've purchased *The Dog Walker's Startup Guide: Create Your Own Lucrative Dog Walking Business in 12 Easy Steps* because you've decided to make an important change in your own life. You want to control your destiny and take responsibility for your own success.

It is through your own efforts that success will be yours. Starting a dog walking business is easy and rewarding in many ways, including financially, but it doesn't happen without personal effort and commitment. In other words, it won't happen by itself. It seems obvious enough, but when you think about it, how many times have we purchased something in the hopes that it would make our lives better and instead it sits collecting dust in our basement? I can show you what to do, but you have to do the work to make it happen.

You also purchased this book because you want to learn from someone who has done the work, made the mistakes, and learned from them. Congratulations, that's a great first step! Dog walking services are in great demand these days, but there is competition. You need to set yourself apart; you need to make sure your phone rings. I am going to show you how. You will have the distinct advantage of building on ideas that have already proven themselves, that have been created through trial and error, and have been field tested for the last seven years.

One thing to start doing right now, wherever you are, is to visualize yourself running your company, having satisfied clients, and making money. Visualize yourself enjoying your business and watching it grow. All creation starts with a thought. You started creating your lucrative and enjoyable business the moment you purchased this book. By implementing the ideas it contains and combining them with creative visualization, positive thinking and, of course, through your own best efforts, that success can be yours. Stay positive, and if you hit a snag, do what the truly successful do when they encounter a setback, thank the world for showing you how *not* to do something! Every setback is a chance to learn something. If the successful treat setbacks like gold, so should you! Remember, "Fortune favors the bold."

My story

I began dreaming about a new life while enduring a grueling ten hour session in a dark editing room in Denver, Colorado. I was the video editor, and in the shadows behind me sat an advertising executive and two creative directors. Literally every edit I made in that thirty second commercial was decided by the committee of dark shapes sitting behind me. When a decision was beyond them, it was escalated to yet another person on the other end of a phone. Occasionally I would offer a suggestion, but more often than not I kept my mouth shut. Why prolong the torture? One session in particular was punctuated by a comment from one of my clients, "How can you stand sitting in this room every day?" That day I realized my dream of becoming a famous director in Hollywood was exactly that—a dream. I really didn't want it, I also realized. The price was too high and I suspected that the prize was illusory. I knew without any doubt that if I didn't get out of that situation it would one day kill me.

There were many options. I could go back to school. I could maneuver for a better and more flexible job within the industry. I could go back to freelancing and perhaps gain the illusion of independence, or I could start my own business. I knew something had to change, but I just wasn't sure where to begin. So, more time passed with me "grudging it out" as a producer and editor. As luck would have it, six months later my wife received a job offer in Massachusetts and I was all to happy to move, leaving Denver and that editing room far behind. With her job secure, we left Colorado. She began her new job and I began searching for my *greener pastures.*

Learned helplessness

They call it "pounding the pavement" and that's what it felt like. With every résumé I mailed out or job interview I landed, I felt a persistent feeling of self-doubt—something wasn't right. I saw in each job, no matter what it was, my inevitable doom. I feared I was headed for another sunless room and a slow but steady slip into depression. I chose to ignore the gnawing feeling a little longer and took a senior editor position for a corporate video production company (think blue plate diners as opposed to four star restaurants). It was a *huge* step back for me, and I quickly surmised that my employer was "Attila the Hun" in an industry of barbarians.

I still can't decide what was worse about that job, my boss Attila, or the dreadful odor in the building. One of the offices must have, at one time, housed a dental clinic. Every day as I entered the building I was greeted by the nausea-inducing smell of professional dental products. It's that sweet, minty, antiseptic odor that in an almost Pavlovian way makes your teeth hurt and your stomach clench. It seemed an appropriate odor considering how unpleasant I found both experiences (the dentist's office and my job). Each day I would drag my feet up the long flight of stairs to my proverbial "dental chair" in front of the editing station—without the benefit of novocaine or laughing gas.

Indeed, many people experience this phenomenon called "learned helplessness." Perhaps you can relate to feeling this way in your own life. An example of it is best illustrated by a well known and diabolical experiment on laboratory rats. A rat was placed inside a box with a metal floor known as a "Skinner Box" named after the psychologist B.F. Skinner who invented the test. Randomly and without warning, an electrical current was sent through the floor of the box and the rat received an electrical shock. At first the rat did what you might expect and tried to escape. But, after a while the rat gave up trying despite the relentless shocks it was receiving. It just lay on the floor without moving, not because it no longer hurt, but because it had accepted that there was nothing he could do about the situation. I didn't need to torture a rat to find evidence of learned helplessness. I needed only to look in the mirror.

My profession had become merely a means to an end—that end was my home and life on the North Shore of Massachusetts. When I was done with my editing for the day, I had an exhausting two hour commute to look forward to, which if I was lucky, would get me home by 7 PM. This new job was wearing me down fast and I was very unhappy. Attila began regularly asking me to stay late to finish "critical" projects and hinted at weekends being the alternative to long days. It was about this time I began to have stress related health issues which required some serious dietary and lifestyle changes. Among other things, I experienced rapid weight loss and difficulty sleeping. On the way home from the doctor's office I remembered my epiphany in the editing room in Denver just a year ago and wondered, "What am I waiting for—an emergency room visit?"

A ray of light

I talked things over with my wife and she suggested, almost jokingly, that I could walk dogs for a living. But it was true genius, and at that moment I immediately saw the potential of her idea. Neither my wife nor I knew of anyone who did this. Walking dogs for a living seemed outlandishly simple and yet extremely vital. For example, if we were going to own a dog as we had always dreamed—and wanted to continue to work and commute far from home—we could not do it without hiring someone to take him out during the day. Since we didn't even consider this was a possibility, we had postponed getting a dog for many years. "How many others like us could benefit from a service of this kind?" I wondered.

I started to work on the idea in the evenings, and a plan for how to make it happen began to emerge. This was a business I knew I could create, and it didn't require bank loans, investors, and lots of capital. It would take some creativity, desire and determination, which I had in spades. My health problems were the tip of an iceberg that had only begun to surface after years of ignoring the warning signs. If I was going to turn my life around, it was up to me!

It is commonly said that when you have a dream and take decisive action to bring it about, the universe bands with you to make that dream a reality. Well, I can tell you it does. This is not some useless platitude, it's the truth. The famous psychologist Carl Jung called it "synchronicity" while others call it serendipity. Whatever you want to call it, a week later it entered my life. I received a phone call from a family member and heard about a producer who was looking for a part-time freelance editor to help her edit her documentary. This turned out to be a wonderful project, and it provided me with the free time and money I needed to develop my dog walking business. I was giddy the day I walked into Attila's office and tendered my resignation.

My journey begins

S tarting this business was a trail blazing experience for me. There were no books or information about it at the time, for it was still in its infancy. I went at it from the perspective of an advertiser. My first steps were to identify the demographic (who might purchase my services) and then build my business identity based on what would appeal to these folks. From there I developed an image that suggested that identity. For Newburyport Walks Dogs it was a bright, friendly, professional image that exuded hope and happiness. The website design reflected this image very well with its clean appearance and the bright happy colors of a sunny day.

I started my advertising efforts with fliers, targeting areas near my own home. Folks who saw my fliers went home and checked out my website. This got me a couple of calls. My first meetings were somewhat awkward, but I got through them. Much to my relief, I found it easy to talk about something that genuinely interested me for a change. People love to talk about their pets, and if you love to talk about animals these conversations flow naturally and easily without much effort. I gained two clients from the fliers and one from a referral. This was a good start but it wasn't nearly enough. I decided to call the city clerk and find out about obtaining a mailing list of residents. It was from that initial call that I learned I could obtain the list of licensed dog owners.

This was a bit of a scary time for me with all the changes in my life and the lost income from leaving my editing position, so getting my hands on this list was really a great thing at the time. I knew if I put my heart into it, I would be able to drum up some business. I dedicated myself to calling 25 people from the list every day. The first 5 were the hardest by far, but the more people I called the better I got at it. As it turned out, making those calls became easy and productive. Each conversation I had with a prospective customer clarified what Newburyport Walks Dogs was going to be and what services I would sell. I compiled a list of frequently asked questions (FAQ) and included it on my website.

So many people wanted me to send them information that through a naturally evolving process "the welcome packet" was born (you will read about it in this book). This packet eventually evolved into a sales tool at client meetings. Soon my schedule began to fill up with dog walks, and as a result my anxiety ebbed. If I had had what you are now holding in your hand—this book—it would have been a lot easier and taken much less time.

So, things were looking up. I still had work to do, but my little business venture was working pretty nicely. I was starting to make good money and best of all: I had escaped Attila the Hun, the dental chair, and four hours of daily commuting. That autumn as I walked down a leaf covered path with a black Lab puppy named Beatrice, I thought about how much my life had changed. How it was not just an idea or a dream anymore, but it had finally happened! The stark contrast to what my life is now, as opposed to then, is astonishing, but it also makes a lot of sense. Having been trapped inside a dark room, the logical answer was to get outside into the sunshine. I created my own dog walking business, and I never once looked back.

How to use this book

As I wrote this book I realized it was going to be important to keep all the suggested resources current. That is always a challenge in publishing, especially when referencing online resources, as links often become outdated or obsolete. I decided to circumvent this issue by referring readers to a "companion site" (*http://www.dogzanny.com*), which will contain links and references to other resources. This way I can keep the information current and add new resources as they become known to me. Each chapter will reference the relevant resources available on the companion site.

I also reference *The Dog Walker's Companion* (DVD), which I created to augment *The Dog Walker's Startup Guide*. Though the book alone provides you with everything you need to start your own business, purchase of the DVD provides additional resources to make your journey even easier. These include: a 20 minute full client interview; basic dog training lessons using reward-based training techniques for commands such as sit, down, sit-stay, down-stay, not jumping up, and leash manners that are particularly useful to dog walkers; business materials including forms, agreements, sample letters, example advertisements, and scripts (you must have a DVD-ROM drive on your computer to access these files). For a complete description of what is contained on the DVD please visit *http://www.dogzanny.com*. Again, you will be reminded of the DVD resources, when appropriate, throughout the book.

The chapters are organized by the order in which they should be read and acted upon for best effect. Fully read each chapter before moving on to the next. Investigate the resources that are recommended and/or find other similar options. At the end of most chapters there is a section called "Take action." Action is the key to making your dream a reality. I have included this section specifically to distill the necessary steps you must take to achieve the goals set forth in each chapter. Before moving on to the next chapter, make plans for when, where, and how you are going to address each of the action items listed.

STEP 1

Projecting Income and Defining Your Business & Services

Chapter Summary

This chapter explores the economics of dog walking and how it relates to your unique financial situation. You will also define what services your business is going to offer and how you will compete with other dog walking businesses in your area. This will require some research into your personal finances and also within the dog walking industry in your area. An honest assessment of your financial situation and needs, as well as how much potential income you can expect from starting your dog walking business, is critical to your success. Knowing exactly how many clients you are going to need to survive doesn't just make good business sense, it will also provide you with peace-of-mind. The following subjects will be covered:

- ▶ How much income you need to meet your lifestyle needs
- ▶ The importance of customer service
- ▶ Some ideas for services
- ▶ Pros and cons of particular services
- ▶ Shopping the competition
- ▶ Figuring out your MTN (minimum target number)

▶ Examples and case studies

▶ Special considerations

How much money do you need?

T here are as many answers to this question as there are people reading this book. Everyone has a unique financial situation that must be considered. In order to arrive at this elusive figure, you're going to have to dig—not only into your financial records, but into your soul as well. How much do you want to work? What are you willing to live without? Can you temper your lifestyle to grow with your business? All these questions will need to be analyzed and answered individually. Being self employed doesn't necessarily mean you get to keep more money! Yes, you get to write off business expenses, but you will need to in order to pay for things like health insurance, liability insurance, and other expenses that are unique to business ownership.

We will be talking about *gross income* in this chapter for simplicity's sake, but gross income is not the same as net income. *Net income after taxes* is the money you receive after taxes and all other business expenses have been paid. It is your take-home pay and/or profits. It is the money you have left over to pay your personal bills, mortgage, and other expenses. *Gross income* is the money the business earns *before* paying its expenses and taxes. You can expect your *net income after taxes* to be anywhere from 20%–50% less than your *gross income*. When figuring out how much gross income you need per month to pay personal expenses you will need to adjust that number to account for taxes and business expenses. For example if you require $2,800 per month to pay your current personal expenses you will probably need to earn at least $4,000 dollars in *gross income* per month. It is impossible to give you a precise number or percentage as there are many factors that determine how much you will need to set aside for taxes and expenses. Businesses with more write-offs pay less tax but pay more in expenses. To get a better idea of what to expect you will need to discuss your situation with a CPA (Certified Public Accountant). A local CPA can be found by searching online, browsing the phone book, or better still, asking a business owner you respect for the name of their accountant!

Putting your financial picture into perspective is easy for some, and hard for others. There are many books on personal finance that will help you get a handle on money, what it is, what it isn't, and how to take control of it instead of being controlled by it! My recommendation is *Your Money or Your Life*, by Joe Dominguez and Vicki Robin. This book suggests looking at your life, assets, and finances in terms of the "life energy" you spend acquiring them—and at the end of it all, what real value they actually have. It is the perfect book for those contemplating starting a business like dog walking.

Customer service

This is what your business really is. You need to understand that although "dog care" is the product you are selling, the success of the business will boil down to customer service. It has been my observation that quality customer service has been on a steady decline. Consumers have become complacent and willing to pay for inferior service in favor of a low price. This complacency has been rewarded with cheap products, unacceptable service, and companies that really don't give a damn. Fortunately for you, many businesses are operating with this mentality which gives you a great opportunity to dazzle your clients with five star services! Your service will far surpass what most people are accustomed to and you will soon have far more clients than you can possibly handle.

What exactly is customer service? Simply put, it is responding to customers' needs either proactively or reactively. Proactive service *anticipates* a customer's needs before there is a problem, while reactive service *responds* to a problem or direct request from a customer as it occurs. Proactive service is arrived at through intuition, creative thought, your past customer service experiences, and feedback from customers. Proactive service is something high-end hotels are famous for. It's why a five star hotel can charge big bucks even though the rooms themselves might not be much different than a three or four star hotel. To define your customer "services" you must put yourself in the customers' shoes, and you must also ask your customers what they want from a dog walking service. Dog walking has its own unique set of challenges for fostering a sense of quality service.

The thing about the dog walking business that makes customer service a bit of a challenge is that you rarely interact with your dogs' owners. The dogs you care for may think you are #1, but your clients don't know that, do they? So, your challenge as a business owner is how to provide your customers with a very personal high-quality service that they are both *aware* of and can *participate* in.

Today's international and national companies can't offer the kind of personalized service your small business can. Most folks' expectations of customer service have been diminished by the kind of one-size-fits-all service they receive from these billion dollar giants. A truly sustainable business is one that provides a service of the highest quality and that says to the consumer: your hard earned money has value to us, and we respect and want to earn that money. The cost-cutters may survive if they are selling nothing but simple quality goods, but service industries whose motto is "lower cost at the price of service" will not survive. That is where you come in. Be the Ritz Carlton of dog walking businesses and wow your clients with five star services!

Take two dog walking businesses, for example. In business 'A' they offer a 20 minute walk, nothing else. Business 'B' offers a 20 minute walk, a weekly blog, a monthly call to "check in" and an à la carte basic obedience training program. Which business would do better? Business B directly benefits the customer and will breed loyalty, generate referrals, and foster a sense of trust and community.

The following items are some ideas for impressing your clients with professionalism and thoughtfulness:

▶ Always answer the phone when it rings, never let it go to voice mail. Always answer your email within a day. Show your customers that you are grateful for their business! Get to know your customers and remember what's important to them.

▶ If a customer tells you in passing that her favorite flowers are daffodils, make a note of it. Then buy her a bouquet of daffodils for her next birthday.

▶ Don't forget the holidays either, a card at the least. If your clients celebrate Christmas, think about a great dog-related gift THEY will enjoy!

▶ Take a *Dale Carnegie* seminar (I did) if you want to learn the secrets of outstanding customer service skills! *http:// www.dalecarnegie.com/*

Some ideas for services

1. **The Dog Walk:** This is the staple service for most dog-walkers. It doesn't require a group of dogs, or a vehicle capable of carrying them. This service lends itself best to the noontime period from 10:30am-2:30pm and serves those looking for a service that gets their dog some fresh air and relief while they are at work. In this service you decide the duration of the walk based in large part on what other dog walking services in your area are doing. You may add services such as plant watering or feeding fish or a cat for an additional fee. It's always a good idea to do a little something extra for your clients at no charge. It could be as simple as taking in a package or the mail. Once you get customers, it will help you to keep them.

2. **Dog Safaris:** This service involves picking up a dog, or preferably several that are social and get along well, and bringing them somewhere fun for dogs, such as a park, beach, or obsta-

cle course. This service can be scheduled any time and works well for early mornings and late afternoons. Be sure you know the rules and regulations regarding dogs for the areas to which you plan on taking them. The focus of this service is mental stimulation and enjoyment. *Dog Safaris* can include exercise, but the focus is on locations and novelty. This should be a service that older dogs would benefit from as well as young active dogs.

3. **Dog Boot Camp:** This service involves anything that gets the dogs' heart rate up. It could be playing ball in the owner's yard, hitching the dogs up to a sled and tearing down a trail, or maybe just going to a park or an active doggy play group. The focus of this service is exercise, so you need to create a safe and lawful environment for dogs to run and get a good work-out. This is a great service for adolescent and adult dogs and fits well into the early morning and late afternoon time frame. This service has a lot of potential as not everyone is capable of exercising their own dogs. The sick, disabled, or elderly dog owners could really use this service!

4. **Play Groups:** This works well if you happen to have a bunch of dogs that all get along well together. Play groups are a lot of fun for dogs, but they do require you to be on your toes and very careful in your supervision of play. It is your responsibility to make sure play doesn't get out of hand and turn into a dog fight. The focus of this service is dog-dog socialization and play. In this service it's a good idea to offer separate groups based on the dogs' ages and sizes. For example, a small dog group, puppy group, or a rough and tumble group of adult

dogs. This service is a great adjunct to a training program and can be scheduled any time.

You will need to consider the area you are working in and decide what will work best for you. Some cities have dog parks where you can take a play group, but rural areas may lack this resource and provide another such as large State Parks or Federal Lands. Do you have unused land that could be fenced in and used for such a purpose? If you do, make sure you inform your neighbors and check city ordinances to see if it's allowed! Again, I suggest scheduling *Dog Safaris, Boot Camp,* and *Play Groups* for off-peak times such as early morning and late afternoons, and leave the noontime hours for basic walks.

Shopping the competition

What types of services are other dog walkers offering and what are they charging for them? Here you will have to pretend you are a potential customer by going through the yellow pages and calling them one by one. Explain that you are thinking about taking a job out of town that will require a long commute and you're researching options. Try to get as much information as you can by telephone. Ask them to mail you any additional information they have on their services. Also, be sure to ask them how long they have been in business. This will help put their pricing in perspective. For example, if someone who has been in business less than a year is charging 30% less than everyone else who has been in business longer, you can assume they are trying to undersell the existing competition in hopes of gaining some market share. Don't try to get market share by becoming a price cutter. It rarely works and only serves to create animosity among your competitors; not to mention, it ruins the market and makes getting a fair payment for services harder for everyone, including you. Instead, define your business through the quality of services you provide. Charge accordingly based on the pricing averages of comparable services offered by other dog walkers and your costs to offer services (your overhead). To make it easier to calculate whether the market price for services will meet your needs, I have created a simple way of breaking it down. The minimum target number (MTN) is the minimum number of walks you require per day to meet your financial needs.

Figuring out your MTN
(Minimum Target Number)

A t this point you should have decided what services you are prepared to offer and what you are going to charge for them. Now you are ready to calculate your MTN, the minimum target number of walks you will need to meet your income needs. The numbers below have been rounded up or down to the nearest dollar. Also, for the sake of simplicity, the businesses in the following examples have no employees. This is the math I use to arrive at the MTN:

1. There are 52 weeks in a year. Subtract two weeks vacation and you have 50 work weeks in which to earn money for a given year.

2. Multiply 50 weeks by 5 (the number of business days in a week), and you get 250 business days per year.

3. Divide 250 by 12 (the number of months in a year) and you get an average of 20.83 business days per month.

4. Now, take the amount of gross income you require per month and divide it by 20.83. The answer you get is how much you must earn per business day to meet your monthly minimum. Make sure you put aside enough money each month to cover your vacation time!

Example

[$2,916 (gross monthly requirement) / 20.83 (business days per month) = $140 (per business day)]

Now to get your MTN, take the amount you are charging per walk (in this case $15), and divide it into $140. [$140 / $15 = 9.33 (MTN)]

Your MTN is between 9-10 walks/clients per business day.

You will need to put aside $28 per week over the next 50 weeks to have enough money saved to cover normal personal expenses during your two weeks of vacation. Use this formula [($140 x 10 (days) = $1,400) / 50 = $28]

The following case studies show how the MTN equation applies to two different dog walking businesses.

Case Study 1: <u>Regal Hounds Dog Walking Service</u>
by Paul
Location: Urban

R egal Hounds is strictly a dog walking business offering group walks in an urban neighborhood. Paul decided to market his business to neighborhoods and specific apartment buildings to minimize travel time and maximize income. Since the service area was condensed, he didn't have any travel time or fuel costs, but he needed significant prep time, as he had to go from apartment to apartment and pick up all the dogs. His largest group was five dogs, and it took him about 30 minutes to get all the dogs together. Based on other dog walking businesses in his area, Paul decided to charge $15 per dog for a 30 minute group walk. He could handle about one group per hour. Thus, Paul was walking five dogs per hour and earning a total of $75 per hour. Paul required $4,000 per month in gross income. So what was Paul's MTN?

▶ Divide $4,000 by 20.83 and you get $192. Paul needs to earn at least $192 per day to meet his expenses.

▶ $192 / $15 (average price for a standard group walk in his area) = 12.8

▶ His MTN is 12.8 dogs per day

▶ With just three group walks consisting of five dogs per group, he is working three hours for a total of $225 per day x 20.83 equals $4,687 per month.

He has more than exceeded his monthly requirement ($4,000) and still has five hours open for more business in an eight hour day. Paul is running a nice business. He has decided to use the extra time to pursue other interests rather than find more clients.

▶ Hiring an employee to increase the number of clients you can handle is quite profitable in this situation, as the amount of business income generated by having an additional person is high. If a group of 5 dogs earns $75 per hour, the wages you pay your employee ($15 per hour as an example) do not cut so deeply into your profits.

Case Study 2: <u>Spots Dog Walking Service</u>
by Jane
Location: Suburban

Spots is a dog walking and/or pet sitting business. Based on other dog walking businesses in her area, Jane decided to charge $15 for a 20 minute walk/visit during peak times (10AM–2PM) and $13 for off-peak. At 20 minutes per walk, she could easily average 2 walks per hour with approximately 20 minutes left over for travel time. The service area was rather spread out, and each dog was walked individually. Thus Jane could individually walk 2 dogs per hour and earn a total of $26–$30 per hour. Jane required at least $3,000 per month in gross income from the business. In order to translate that amount into a number she could work with and compare with her competition, she needed to break things down to the day.

Example

▶ Divide $3,000 by 20.83 and you get $144. So she needs to earn at least $144 per day to meet her expenses.

▶ $144 / $15 (average price for a standard walk in her area) = 9.6

▶ Her MTN is 9.6 walks per day at $15 per walk

But Jane can only walk a maximum of 8 dogs at peak times (10AM–2PM). She will need to make up the difference at off-peak times.

▶ (Peak time):   8 walks x $15 = $120

▶ (Off-peak):   2 walks x $13 = $26

▶ Total: = $146

Her MTN is really 8 peak time plus 2 off-peak time walks.

At two walks per hour she is working for a total of five hours per day to achieve her MTN. She could increase her monthly income without needing to hire additional help by finding clients who will settle for off-peak times. She may want to think about marketing additional services such as *Doggie Play Groups* or *Dog*

Safaris to her clients so that she can maximize the amount of money she makes per hour and take advantage of slow periods in the day. She could also consider charging more by finding ways to make her service better than her competitors.

Either way, that's a lot of walks. If you have extra pounds you need to shed, you'll be shedding them. Your income is determined by the number of walks you can do in a day and/or cluster together into group activities.

Considerations

O nce you have done these calculations for your own business, you should have a pretty good idea how many clients you will need and how much to charge for your services. You don't need to live in an urban environment to do what Paul did. For those living in suburban areas, you'll probably have a bit more travel; getting groups together may involve a little more salesmanship and effort, but look at it as a fun challenge. *Dog Safaris* and *Play Groups* are great for this purpose.

For those of you in urban areas, don't sweat not being able to offer *Dog Safaris*. I know of one dog walker in New York City who walks three groups of dogs (six dogs in each group) and charges $15 per dog. She makes around $70,000 per year! Not too bad considering she works only about four hours a day.

When interviewing clients, ask them what would be the ideal time for you to come walk their dog. Make sure they know you will come as close to that "target" time as possible, but that due to an ever changing schedule you can't guarantee a specific time for everyone. Promise them you will be able to arrive within an hour of the target time in most cases. What I did in my business is offer time "zones" for walks with tiered pricing for each. For example, peak times were between 10:30AM–2:30PM weekdays. Then there was off-peak, which was 8:00AM–10:30AM and 2:30PM–6:00PM weekdays. This billed slightly lower than peak time. Evenings, weekends and holidays billed the highest.

▶ *Play Groups, Group Walks* and *Dog Safaris* are the most time effective and income producing services you can offer if you live in an area that supports it.

▶ Individual walks involve the most time and effort on your part for the least return.

Take action

1. Read some personal finance books such as, *Your Money or Your Life*, by Joe Dominguez and Vicki Robin.

2. Determine what your monthly personal expenses are and add them up. Consider what expenses can be eliminated (trim the fat) and then add up what remains. This is the amount of net income your business must earn per month to support your current lifestyle.

3. Make an honest financial self-assessment right now by answering the following questions: Do you have enough money set aside to cover your personal expenses for the next six months while you get your business up and running? Can you work part-time? What other options do you have? Can you

live with a friend for a while? Move out of your home and rent a studio?

4. Contact a CPA once you've compiled all your financial information to get a professional opinion.

5. Call the competition. Find out what services they offer and what they charge for them.

6. Brainstorm what services you can offer. Use my examples or come up with your own. Get creative!

7. Determine your MTN using the formulas I have provided. Decide if the services you intend to offer meet or exceed your MTN.

8. Take the numbers you used to figure out your MTN and project how much income you expect your business to earn in the next 6 and 12 months. Figure a best case and worst case scenario for each.

9. Take your projections and talk with your accountant. Find out roughly how much in taxes you will need to pay. Talk with him about the advantages and disadvantages of a home office as it pertains to your situation.

10. Educate yourself in any areas in which you feel you are weak. Consider enrolling in a business, customer service, or financial planning course or seminar. I took a *Dale Carnegie seminar*, which has helped me immeasurably in this business.

STEP 2

The Business of Dog Walking

Chapter Summary

A dog walking business is like any other business in that its function for you, the business owner, is to provide an income source. Therefore, like all businesses, you as the owner must be aware of the small details that will make your business successful. This chapter discusses many important aspects of business ownership, which, if considered carefully, will strengthen your business and provide a solid foundation upon which to build. The following subjects will be covered:

- ▶ Naming your business
- ▶ Business entities
- ▶ Licenses
- ▶ The *Better Business Bureau*
- ▶ Insurance and professional memberships
- ▶ Service agreements
- ▶ Creating marketing materials and *welcome packet*
- ▶ Home offices
- ▶ Tracking business performance
- ▶ Keeping track of paperwork
- ▶ Other topics that will protect and support your business

Having things in order from the beginning will save you time and confusion later on. Let's get started!

Name your business

This is a simple one—not really. Make sure your business name conveys the nature of your business. Try to restrain yourself from using cutesy names. They don't really convey professionalism and tend to marginalize your business as some kind of little project or pastime. Also, you might want to include the area or city name in your business name, as this will promote a feeling of familiarity and even a little trust in your potential customers. I used *Newburyport Walks Dogs*. Try to create a name that will encapsulate your business model.

Create a legal business entity

Decide on what type of company it will be: sole proprietorship, LLC, S-Corp. etc., and get competent legal and financial advice if necessary. It is beyond the scope of this book to offer advice on specific legal and financial advantages for each type of business. It will depend on the complexity of your business model and how it will grow in the coming years. There are a great many books that provide tons of information, but in the end they still leave the decision squarely in your hands. Why? Because every business is different, even two businesses that do the same things. Contact a good attorney and describe your business model; she will be able to explain the advantages and disadvantages for your particular business.

Licenses

Your state and town or city will likely require that you file for a business license. Once you have registered your name with the state and filed your paperwork establishing your business entity, go ahead and get your town/city license (your lawyer may include this as part of her service). It doesn't require anything special and the license doesn't really mean anything. It doesn't bear the same significance as a license to practice medicine does. It's just a way for the city/town to track who is doing business there.

The Better Business Bureau

You might want to become a member of the *BBB*. For new businesses, being a member of the *BBB* is a great way to engender a sense of trust. Having this logo on your website and advertising material goes a long way. After all, the *BBB*'s slogan is "Start with trust."

Insurance & professional memberships

You need to protect yourself and your business in the event that you are sued. Liability insurance for your business can be obtained privately or through membership with one of the following national pet sitting associations.

▶ *NAPPS, www.petsitters.org* (annual fee, insurance is additional)

▶ *PSI, www.petsit.com* (annual fee, insurance is additional)

▶ *PSA, www.petsitllc.com* (annual fee, insurance is included)

Membership in a professional organization increases your credibility and can make you a better dog walker and pet sitter through your interactions with other dog walkers and sitters. Those who are just starting out and have little or no professional pet-care experience would be well advised to join one (for the insurance at the least). The pet care industry is evolving quickly. Becoming a member enables you to influence and shape the industry as well as benefit from the combined experience of many others. Check out what each has to offer and decide what works best for you. Make copies of your insurance certificate and association membership and include it in the *welcome packet* (described later) you bring with you to new client interviews.

Bonding may be included in your insurance plan. Bonding is not insurance. It protects the client from dishonest acts by an employee of your company (such as theft) only if they are convicted of the crime. Once convicted, the bonding company will pay your client for the loss (usually their homeowners insurance deductible, if insured). Then the bonding company will go after the person they bonded (your employee) to recover the money. If you bond *yourself* the client can be assured that they will be paid if *you* are convicted. Another thing to check for is whether the insurance company offers to pay for replacing the locks on a customer's home should you lose their house key. I've never had to file that claim, but it's conceivable that you could have to. It's a good indicator that the insurance provider has a well researched policy to offer.

Your service agreement

I have included a sample agreement from my own business at the end of this chapter for informational purposes. It is important to make sure your contract is created by a lawyer who works in and understands the laws of your state. Your contract should be a legally binding document. The only way to be sure of that is to have it drawn up by your own lawyer. Show my agreement to your lawyer for review. She can take the essence of it and make a legally sound document that will protect you and your business.

▶ A printable version of the sample service agreement, in PDF format, can be found on *The Dog Walker's Companion* (DVD), available for purchase from *http://www.dogzanny.com*.

Creating your welcome packet

Y our welcome packet is where to describe your services and policies in detail for the customer. It will include information about your background, references, licenses, insurance certificates, rate plans, detailed descriptions of services, forms, promotional gifts, and other information useful to your customers. This well-organized packet will demonstrate to your client that you are serious about walking dogs. By taking the time to include any information or materials that the client could want when evaluating your business and services, you ensure that you make the best first impression you possibly can.

► Sample items for a welcome packet can be found on *The Dog Walker's Companion* (DVD).

Organize your information and papers neatly, and in a well-conceived way. Be sure to include headings, sub headings and bullets so as to lead the reader through your documents. You don't want them to be staring at a wall of text. You may use clip art, but be careful about the quality of the art and how much you use. Most of the pre-bundled clip art looks pretty unprofessional and won't impress anyone. If you have exceptional clip art and want to use it here and there to add some color and interest to your documents, by all means do so. If you aren't really design oriented I suggest leaving the clip art out. To be honest, I think most (if not all) clip art is cheesy, but then again my background is in advertising and marketing.

Once you have completed your documents, you can bind them yourself in a fairly nice professional report folder. These can be purchased at any office supply store. Another option is to have them professionally bound at your local print shop. I suggest binding them yourself, at least to start with. Control costs as much as you can when starting out!

Step 1: Your "About Page" should have the following elements

1. **What you've done:** One paragraph of text describing what you've been doing. A summary of the last 10 years would be fine. It is basically a condensed résumé in readable form. It is okay if you were a sales rep, lawyer, real estate agent, and hair stylist so long as you can convince your

potential client how those skills can contribute, or have led to creating your business as a dog walker. You don't have to have an extensive background in animal care, though it doesn't hurt. I started my business after being a producer and editor in the film and television industry! This is where credibility indicators come into play, as you will see in the next paragraph. Focus on any pet care experience you've had, including your own pets.

2. **What you've learned:** Include such things as memberships and affiliations with known organizations, training certificates, and education. Classes taken that relate to animals but did not lead to certificates or diplomas should also be mentioned. Your experience in personal dog ownership counts. Don't forget the time you have donated at the local animal shelter!

3. **The synthesis:** Discuss how your prior work and education have led you to start your dog walking business. Tell about how you've always had a desire to work with animals and how your life has prepared you for that task. Give a hopeful view for the future and how you plan to provide the best possible service to your clients.

4. **A flattering photograph:** Make the photo a part of the about page by having it printed along with the text. A nice photo of you with your own dog is ideal. Puppies are always a good bet too. Don't staple or tape a loose photograph to the page!

Step 2: Copies of important documents

▶ Business licenses

▶ Insurance certificate

▶ Other relevant certificates (training programs, *Red Cross Pet First Aid*, memberships such as the *Better Business Bureau*, pet sitting associations, etc.)

Step 3: Full descriptions of your services and pricing

▶ This is fairly straightforward. Lay your services out on paper, emphasizing the products that you feel are the most popular. Be sure to put the most desired and profitable service plan at the top of the page and indicate that it is the "best value." Cell phone and cable companies are great examples of how tiered service plans are used to compete against one another and sell the best value plan. Visit a few providers online and check out the service plans they offer. They usually offer several plans that range in cost and services provided, but there will always be a "featured" plan which may be labeled as the "best value." Why reinvent the wheel? Learn from the pros and design your plans in the same way!

▶ Try to keep to a one-page summary of your services and rates in a clear, well-designed format. Include contact information. Make sure you include an "effective" date range or season. Some examples:

Effective Spring 2008

Good through December 2008

▶ Include a disclaimer that indicates that rates are subject to change without notice.

Step 4: Agreements, forms, coupons, business cards, and promotional gifts

▶ Include 2 copies of the customer agreement, one for you and one for the customer. Include any other forms you might need such as the customer information form.

▶ Bring several "Good Neighbor" coupons with you. Offer a 20% discount on the first week of service—your client will love to give these away to her friends and neighbors! It's a fantastic way to advertise. When your client gives away a coupon to a friend, you get a new client and your neighbor looks like a philanthropist!

▶ Bring 2-3 business cards. They will be kept by the client long after your other materials have found their way into a forgotten drawer.

▶ If you've created any advertising gifts such as magnets, pens, or notepads, include one with your packet.

Step 5: Local information

▶ Here I would include any information of value to dog owners that doesn't directly compete with your own business.

Your clients will appreciate the information, and it will add direct value to your welcome packet. Descriptions of local parks (hours and leash laws), doggy events, pet stores that sell quality dog foods, and other types of services will all be welcome information. Also, provide your clients with the low-down on the best times and locations for meeting up with other dog owners and play groups (special insider knowledge). You can even set up business advertising partnerships with local dog-related businesses (vets, groomers, pet stores), where you promise to provide information about them to your clientele in return for discounts and in-kind advertising on their end.

Home office

You may take a home office deduction if you have a section of your home that you can devote solely for business use. You don't have to devote an entire room for business use in order to take this deduction. If you have a desk and computer where you conduct business tasks and another section of the room for private use, you can measure the area you use for your business and determine its square footage, which will then enable you to determine the percentage of your home that is for business use. The following text is taken directly from the IRS website and was current as of early 2008:

If you use a portion of your home for business purposes, you may be able to take a home office deduction whether you are self-employed or an employee. Expenses that you may be able to deduct for business use of the home may include the business portion of real estate taxes, mortgage interest, rent, utilities, insurance, depreciation, painting and repairs.

You can claim this deduction for the business use of a part of your home only if you use that part of your home regularly and exclusively:

- As your principal place of business for any trade or business
- As a place to meet or deal with your patients, clients or customers in the normal course of your trade or business

Generally, the amount you can deduct depends on the percentage of your home that you used for business. Your deduction will be limited if your gross income from your business is less than your total business expenses.

If you use a separate structure not attached to your home for an exclusive and regular part of your business, you can deduct expenses related to it.

There are special rules for qualified daycare providers and for persons storing business inventory or product samples.If you are self-employed, use Form 8829 to figure your home office deduction and report those deductions on line 30 of Schedule C, Form 1040.

If you are an employee, you have additional requirements to meet. The regular and exclusive business use must be for the convenience of your employer.

For more information see IRS Publication 587, Business Use of Your Home, available at IRS.gov or by calling 800-TAX-FORM (800-829-3676).

Talk with your accountant about the particulars. He will be able to help you set up your business so that it will meet the standards set by the IRS.

Recording payments

E nter checks into a ledger or financial program like *Quicken*. Keep track of all your receipts for anything business related: all invoices for advertising, web hosting fees, legal fees, accounting fees, software, paper, ink, special clothing, equipment, etc. If you have decent credit, consider obtaining an *American Express* card and using that for all your business purchases. *American Express* makes obtaining year-end reports on spending easy. You can download your statements as tab delimited files to import into spreadsheets and even into *Quicken*. Also remember to keep track of your mileage. There is the usual standard business vehicle deduction (currently 50.5 cents per mile); but there are alternative ways that may prove useful by reducing the amount of paperwork you must keep, or enabling larger deductions, depending on how your car is used for business purposes. Based on the use of your vehicle, your accountant will know the best way for you to take the deduction.

Tracking your business performance

If you don't stay on top of all the changes your clients make, you will wind up forgetting something along the way. The method I used for keeping track of walks, for both record keeping purposes as well as to avoid missing them, was to use a hand-held PDA (personal digital assistant). I would add appointments on the fly, change them, or delete them depending on the messages and notes left for me by my clients. I would then synchronize my PDA with my computer and calendar to update them with all the changes. At the end of the year, I would simply export the data into a spreadsheet and then I was able to sort the data by dates, clients, tags, and other information. When it came time to do taxes, it was a big help because all the records of walks were already recorded without having to do any additional work. That is until I had a catastrophic hard drive failure which may or may not have been the result of some kind of computer virus. The lesson here... BACK UP YOUR DATA!

Most computers come with a CD-RW (write capable drive) these days which can be used to back up your data to a CD-ROM. Other common options include a DVD-RW drive which is capable of storing much more data than a CD-ROM. A portable USB "stick" drive is another option. All can be damaged by mishandling, so store them in a safe place.

Accounting software generally includes charting and tracking capabilities and can generate very detailed reports such as bar graphs, pie charts, or hard data. For example, you can see which clients are your biggest income sources, which are your least productive and all the others in-between. You can analyze an advertising campaign's impact by reviewing these records by date ranges to determine how many new clients you received for your advertising dollars—and how long it will take to recoup the expense!

Keeping track of paper

K eep your customer contact sheets and agreements together and in alphabetical order so they are easy to reference. Be sure to update the information annually so it stays current for your regular customers. Go so far as to put that date in your calendar so you will not forget.

▶ *Last week in March: Update customer contact info.*

Keep all annual business files in a yearly folder. You can buy an accordion style folder with compartments from A-Z for about $7.00 at your local office supply store. Keep all your bills and receipts, letters, and other relevant paper related to that fiscal year in that file folder. At the end of the year, buy a new one and start over. It makes going back as easy as pulling out the prior year's folder.

Take action

1. Naming your business seems deceptively easy. Now is the time to make a decision. What's it going to be?

2. Research and purchase computer accounting software such as *QuickBooks* or *Microsoft Money* and talk to your accountant about setting it up for your business.

3. Hit the office supply store and purchase anything you need for the business. Some items to consider are:

   ▶ Folders (for the *welcome packet*)
   ▶ Accordion file folder
   ▶ Ledgers
   ▶ Envelopes (for direct mail)
   ▶ Paper (for direct mail)
   ▶ Extra ink cartridges for your printer
   ▶ A receipt book
   ▶ Notebooks (for clients)
   ▶ Notepads (for taking notes at client interviews)

4. Check out the companion site for links to great house key organizers or check out your local hardware store (office supply stores may also have something).

5. Consider getting a business credit card such as American Express.

6. Set up a space to do your work. Fill it with positive and motivating materials. Keep it clean and well organized. It's a pleasure to sit down at a clean desk without any clutter. You will get more done in less time. Don't forget, you can take a home office deduction.

7. Talk with your lawyer about setting up a business entity and other legal issues such as your service agreement and state/local business licenses. Print the PDF version of the service agreement included on the DVD if you've purchased it, or make a copy of the one in this book so she has something to go by.

8. Contact your local town/city clerk and find out about getting a business license if you need to do that on your own.

9. Visit the Better Business Bureau online and consider joining. *http://www.bbb.org*

10. Visit the pet sitting associations listed in this chapter and consider joining one. By doing so, you may have access to liability insurance coverage.

11. Start working on your welcome packet. This can be one of the hardest things to sit down and do! Do the easy things first to get things rolling. Set aside a block of time each day for doing this so you can avoid the procrastination trap.

12. Contact the printer you have selected and get any materials you will need printed (business cards, fliers, coupons, and imprinted gifts).

SERVICE AGREEMENT FOR NEWBURYPORT WALKS DOGS

I/We_____ (hereinafter referred to as "Client") have employed Newburyport Walks Dogs (hereinafter referred to as "Service Provider") to provide the following services _____
_____(hereinafter referred to as "Services").

Fees: Fees shall be $_____ for____Services per_____ (week, day, month). Payments are to be made to Service Provider and given to Service Provider on the day services commence for the given period stated in this agreement unless otherwise agreed upon by both parties in writing as an addendum to this Agreement. Twenty four hours advanced notice is required for cancellations and reimbursement. If cancellation is made with less than twenty four hours notice no reimbursement will be made. If Service Provider must take legal action to collect any outstanding balances, and I/We Client are found at fault I/We agree to pay all costs, including attorney's fees, to do so.

Description of Services: I/We Client understand that Service Provider will care for my animal(s) in my absence and this care may require access to my home(s). This care is valid only for animals and is not provided for persons. This animal care may include the following: feeding, providing water, walking my dog(s), providing love and affection to my animal(s), treats, administering medications, providing emergency medical treatment, transportation, admittance to a veterinarians clinic or animal hospital, training, behavioral modification, and any other services which may be required to carry out the duties set forth herein. Service Provider will make all reasonable efforts to provide for the safety and well being of your animal(s) but makes no guarantees that such efforts will be sufficient in all circumstances.

Responsibility/Release and Assumption of Risk: Client acknowledges that the Services offered may be an activity in which damage or injury to animal(s) and/or persons may occur. Client will assume full financial responsibility for the actions of their animal(s). I/We Client understand and are aware that the Services described in this Agreement contain inherent risks and dangers which could result in injury and/or damage to and/or by Client's animal(s) which may arise resulting from, but not limited to, the hazards of all types of traffic, dangerous dogs and animals, interaction with people and other animals, dog aggression, dog attacks, injury to animals or persons, exposure to areas with novel or unfamiliar stimulus, all types of weather and/or unsafe conditions, the hazards of caring for injured, sick or elderly animals, the dangers of civil disturbance, the forces of nature, the negligent or reckless acts or omissions of, and/or the bankruptcy, insolvency or cessation of services by veterinarians, the Service Provider's employees or it's subcontractors.

In consideration of, and as part of the payment for the Services provided herein, I/We Client have and do hereby expressly assume all of the above risks. The terms of this agreement shall serve as a release and express assumption of risk for myself, my animal(s), my heirs, assignees, administrators, executors, and all members of my family, including any minors. I have read and fully understand the provisions and the legal consequences of this Release and Assumption of Risk and I hereby agree to all its conditions, especially noting and agreeing to the release of the Service Provider and its agents, employees, officers, directors, associates, affiliated companies, subcontractors, and related individuals to the extent permitted by law, from liability for injury or damage to or by our animal(s), and assume all risks thereof and full financial responsibility for the actions of my animal(s).

Severability: If any provision of this agreement is deemed to be unenforceable for any reason, this will not affect the validity and enforceability of any other provision of this Agreement.

Termination: Either Client or Service Provider has the right to terminate this Agreement at any time by notice to the other. Client acknowledges that Services will cease upon termination of this Agreement.

This Agreement supersedes all other agreements, written or oral, between Client and Service Provider. This contract for services shall be governed by the laws of the Commonwealth of Massachusetts and enforced in the Massachusetts Courts.

Executed on this_____day of_____, 2_____

"Client"   "Service Provider"

_____   _____
(print name)   (print name)

_____   _____
(signature)   (signature)

STEP 3

Creating a Website

Chapter Summary

Nearly every business these days has its own website. Unfortunately, many websites are actually hindering the success of the businesses they serve, rather than helping. Many business owners overlook the importance of a quality website and don't take the development and maintenance of it seriously—as a result, its appearance winds up looking unprofessional, and its content stale and unremarkable. This chapter will explore the myriad of benefits of having a quality website and why it's critical that you take the time to make your website stand out. Equipped with the information contained in this chapter your website will not only stand out, it might just bring in more business than you can handle at first, so beware! Be sure to check out the companion site *http://www.dogzanny.com* for additional information and direct access to some of the services mentioned in this chapter. The following subjects will be covered:

▶ The purpose a website serves and how will it benefit your business

▶ Ideas that will make your site stand out and add to your customers' experience

▶ Syndicating news feeds to and from your site

▶ Adding discussion forums

▶ Making sure your website design matches your business's personality

▶ Having your site created and designed by someone else

▶ Designing and creating your site yourself

How will it function for my business?

A website is not an option, it's a necessity. Your website will serve as a brick and mortar alternative. Brick and mortar is a term that is used to differentiate a business that offers products through retail stores versus online stores (virtual stores). Your online business presence helps to create a sense of reliability and credibility by supplying your customers with a place to find you, if only virtually. Most people are much more willing to do business with a company that has committed itself to the community by renting office space and/or having a store there. Having a commercial office isn't necessary to running your dog walking business nor is it cost effective. A website is really the next best thing. Think of your website as your virtual storefront.

A website is also a repository of information and communication. When potential customers are introduced to your business either through advertising or word-of-mouth, they can visit your website and get more information about your products and services without having to wait or to talk to you directly. They can in effect, window-shop. From your site they can:

▶ Learn about you, your experiences and credibility.

▶ Make value judgments based on the site and the information contained therein.

▶ Obtain pricing information and schedules.

▶ Find your contact information.

▶ Learn new ideas, information, tips, and other resources that can help pet owners.

Think of your site as a non-linear advertising brochure. You want it to be tantalizing, easy to navigate, and above all, clear and well designed. You want to engage the viewer's imagination; you want to call attention to ideas and concepts of interest to them.

A very good technique worth considering is adding valuable information free of charge. Such information might be tips, recommendations and ideas for dealing with problem behaviors, dog-related news, reviews of products and the like. Offering information is a great way to build interest and a loyal readership for your site. You can consider offering this information as an *RSS feed*, which can further enhance your website's readership and appeal. RSS stands for Really Simple Syndication, and your web designer will be able to set your site up to offer an RSS feed very easily (remember the *simple* part of RSS). An RSS feed is basically a news channel to your blog. Subscribers to your feed get your latest posts delivered directly to them. You might even want to add a forum component for dog owners to find and create doggy play groups, training groups, and other interests. The more traffic your site gets, the more business you get!

Define your business personality

Make sure your website and all of your promotional materials visually reflect the personality of your business. For instance, you don't want to hire a web designer with an ultramodern portfolio if you are going for a classical look. Are you laid back and relaxed slope-side, offering doggy daycare to vacationing Hollywood types in Aspen, Colorado? Or are you running a tight and reliable operation for 9-5ers in a suburb of Chicago? Remember who your audience is! Based on the demographics of the readership of *The Bark* Magazine (2008), the median household income of their readership is $85,000, 72% have college degrees, 89% use email at work or home, and 92% feel that supporting a local dog-friendly business is very important. You should probably cater to that demographic. Think polished and professional. I'm not talking about a cold, sterile corporate appeal but something clean and well put together. Please be sparing with the little pawprint backgrounds and animated yellow puppy dogs, or better yet, avoid them altogether. They are cute and fun but not so reflective of a professional and dependable business.

How do you make it happen?

There are many ways of going about creating a website. The easiest and most costly is to hire a full service web development company to develop the site per your specifications. Another way is by hiring a freelance web designer.

A full service web development team can be a good but expensive option. They will take your site from concept through the design process, and finally through development and hosting it live. If your budget is tight, ask to see what kind of pre-build design options they have. Most will offer an array of semi-custom designs that would probably work very well for your business and will save a lot of time and money versus building it all from scratch. Freelance web designers don't have the overhead these big companies have, and may offer comparable services at a fraction of the cost. Contact at least 3 designers and 3 web development companies and obtain quotes from each. Make sure to ask to see examples of their work that closely resemble what you are trying to create for your site. *Craigslist* is a great place to find hungry freelance web designers. To be honest, a dog walking business website should be exceedingly simple for an experienced web designer to create, including the additions of a blog and user forum (see Step 12).

Doing it yourself

Several website hosts offer do-it-yourself website creation tools that do not require any technical knowledge. This may be a good option to simply get your site up and running for the short term until you can afford to have it redesigned more professionally. If you would like to go this route, you can visit the companion site for links to such hosts.

For you technically literate folks, I suggest using the hosts listed on the companion site and then customizing the services and software the way you like it. There is a learning curve, but if you are fairly computer literate and know your way around *Pho-*

toshop, *Flash*, and *Dreamweaver*, you shouldn't have too much trouble. Visit one of the low cost web hosts listed in the resources section of the companion site to get your domain and hosting. Getting RSS, a forum, and your blog set up will take some time and tinkering, but it's certainly doable. I've done it myself, and it's just a matter of understanding that you will be spending a lot of time reading and researching. Perhaps the best part of doing it yourself is being able to change the design whenever you wish, without having to dip into your wallet every time you do! Just remember, the time you spend on getting the site up and running is time you could be spending getting clients and walking dogs. Get some quotes from professionals and compare that to the time it would take you. Having it done professionally and then requesting all the files and maintaining the site yourself might be a better option.

Take action

1. Decide on the "look" you want your business to have. Visit some of your favorite websites. What do you find visually appealing about them? How have they organized content? Make notes and a list of sites you like and why. You will need this if you hire a web designer to design your site. This information will give them an idea of what you're looking for.

2. Decide if you will be creating a low-cost website using simple but limited online creation tools, hiring a professional to do the work, or doing it yourself using your own web development expertise.

3. Visit the resources section of the companion site for links to services, hosts, and software to get you started. *http://www. dogzanny.com/resources*

4. If you are hiring professionals to create the site, be sure to see samples of their work and make sure it reflects the style you are going for. Get cost estimates from at least three freelancers and three web development companies to compare.

5. Search online for dog walking and pet sitting services and check out their web sites. Some are really nice, others not so nice. Make sure your site looks top notch if you want to stand out.

6. Create the written content for your site. You'll want to provide information about you, your services, service area, rates, contact information, policies, and any other information that would be useful to a potential customer. Include pictures of yourself with dogs and be sure to have an "about me" page.

STEP 4

Advertising Your Business

Chapter Summary

T hink of advertising as your business partner. You can't do anything without it. A lot of people try to start a business and under-fund their advertising budget. Fortunately, you have chosen a business with low startup costs and zero inventory, so you can pour all your capital into advertising. This chapter describes the most accessible and useful forms of advertising available to your business and the advantages of each. The following subjects will be covered:

► Business telephone directory ads

► Newspaper advertising

► Direct marketing

► Mass mail advertising

► Advertising on *Craigslist*

► Door knob hangers

► Creating and distributing fliers

► Car tagging

► Promotional items

► Internet advertising

Business telephone directory

The first thing to do is contact the largest and most popular
business telephone directory for your area and negotiate a
listing agreement. Begin by calling the sales department and ask
for a sales person that handles your region. Ask them to email you
a rate card, and then review the advertising options before calling
back to discuss anything with them. You will want more than a
"one line listing," especially when you are just starting out. So,
look at all the ad options and choose one that will stand out. More
business will come to you via the yellow pages than practically
any other way. It's passive advertising, and it works.

When you are talking to the salesperson, show an interest in
the ad type that is priced one or two steps below the one you are
interested in. They will always try to "bump you up" to the next
level. This is a negotiating strategy. This way you can accept the
bump-up, but only *if* they are willing to give a significant discount! Make sure you seem really reluctant and keep asking for
information about the lower tiers to make them sweat it a little. Do
not accept the rate card as the definitive price, it NEVER is, even
if they assure you it is. It may be that you are calling well ahead of
the rush and they may be reluctant to give away deals at that moment. Ask them when the cut-off for advertising is and tell them
that you will get back to them before that date. In fact the cut-off
they'll tell you on the phone is probably not the real cut-off. It's
been my experience that it's usually about 30-60 days past what
they tell you it is.

If you're fearless, you can hold off until the sales people are
in the "red zone" and they'll give away the ads for a song in most

cases. I say fearless because the "red zone" is the last few weeks before the advertising sales cut-off, and because you are guessing the true cut-off date, it is a gamble, and you risk missing it. However, if you guessed right, you may get a great discount! Sales people have very little to lose by trying to pack as many advertisers in before the cut-off. The idea is that selling off the ads cheaply to motivate reluctant business owners earns them at least some small commission rather than nothing at all. That's why ad sales people keep the true cut-off secret! Be careful though, you don't want to miss the cut-off and lose out on a year of advertising. Here is an example of a business directory ad:

JILL'S DOG WALKING SERVICE

Jill's Dog Walking Service

Give ol' Fido a break. A walk is all it takes.

**Dog Walking - Pet Sitting - Kennel Alternative
Training & Behavior Modification**

Insured, References, Red Cross Pet First Aid Certified

**(999) 222-1111
jill@example.com**

Bottom line, you'll always get a better deal by negotiating. Do not accept the first price they give you. Cite that you are a new customer and ask them to grant you a discount on that basis if for no other reason. You will in all likelihood get one. If they are really stubborn, tell them you will shop elsewhere, but leave your number with them and let them know you would love to advertise with them if they are willing to provide a better price. Hang up. Look at the next largest directory and do the same thing. If you have no luck getting the price you want from either of them, swallow your pride, go with the most popular book, and take the advertising you can afford. Also, make sure your advertising comes with an online listing in their e-directory!

Newspapers

C ontact your local newspaper and obtain an advertising rate card. You will be assigned an Account Executive, or AE. As the success of your advertising can often depend on your AE, determine whether you'll be able to work with this person. A good AE should be responsive and genuinely interested in seeing your business succeed. If they are hard to reach, very slow returning calls, or don't seem to understand what your business is about, then I'd consider finding someone else. Call back the main number, request to speak with the General Manager or Sales Manager, and ask them to reassign your account. Be careful though. If you get a reputation as a pain in the rear, you won't get many breaks from people.

Newspaper advertising operates the same way as business telephone directories—the more money you have to spend on advertising, the greater discounts they can offer. Ask for a "new advertiser" discount. You probably won't get volume discounts yet. Listen to their advice if you aren't marketing savvy. They know what sells and what doesn't. Explain that you are on a limited budget (they will figure that out anyway) and ask what type of ad will provide the most for your money. Remember the old saying, "You get what you pay for"? Do not compromise or cut corners— you will only diminish your own success by doing so. Discuss your options and make sure that if the newspaper offers an online adjunct to print advertising, you get a concurrent listing in both. Here is an example of a simple classified ad:

```
┌────────────────────────────────────────┐
│           Doug's Dog Dating Service      │
│    Everything from dog walking to play-dates │
│    We also offer dog-friendly training programs │
│    Insured, references, pet first aid certified │
│                (999) 222-1111            │
│               www.example.com            │
└────────────────────────────────────────┘
```

Direct marketing

Direct marketing is a method of advertising which markets products and services directly to an individual consumer or group rather than through the use of mass media (radio, print, TV). It is most commonly done through telemarketing or mail. The method I chose for my business was a telemarketing campaign, because it is fast, inexpensive, and effective.

The first thing you must do is obtain the list of dog license holders for your area (to which you are entitled through the Freedom of Information Act) from your local city/town hall. There may be a small administrative fee. Try to obtain an electronic version so you can easily import the data into a mail-merge program and easily print mailing labels. Some towns/cities will only offer you a printed version. The list should contain telephone numbers, dogs' names, breeds, and owners' names and addresses.

Next, you should decide if you will be attempting a telemarketing campaign or direct mail. When I did my calling campaign, the Federal Trade Commission (FTC) had not yet implemented the Do Not Call Registry (DNCR), so it had not been something I needed to consider. Unfortunately, the DNCR will affect who you can call. Any persons who have placed their telephone number in this registry cannot legally be called by a business selling goods and services (there are some exceptions). Fines for calling persons registered with the DNCR can be $11,000 per violation. The calling campaign I am suggesting is considered a telemarketing campaign by the FTC and thus subject to the DNCR. Please visit *http://www.donotcall.gov/* for more information.

It is your responsibility to make sure the numbers you call are not on the registry. Carefully review what the FTC expects of you. Then ask yourself how time- and cost-effective this will be for you. If you plan on doing a telemarketing campaign, be sure to cross check your dog owner list against the DNCR. Mark those telephone numbers which are registered with the DNCR in red, and do not call them.

A telemarketing campaign can generate business quickly and cheaply, but it takes some courage. I know, I know, many of you are balking right now, imagining the sour faces of the people you call or the nasty response you might get. I had the same trepidation when I started making the calls, but it's not that bad. I only got a few hang ups and a couple of rude people. First, you will introduce yourself as a local "smallville" or "yourcityname" business. Right there, they quickly adjust their level of indignation. Plan on calling at least 25 people a day for 10 days. That's 250 people who will know about you by day 10. Continue to make the calls until you are finished with the list. The following is an example calling script.

Calling Script

"Hello?"

"Hello, my name is _____ and I own a dog care business here in _____ called _____. I was wondering if it would be all right if I send you some information about our services?"

"You're a dog walking service?"

"Yes , that's right."

"How did you know we had a dog?"

"We obtained your name through the list of dog owners licensed in (name of town). We are using this list to let local dog owners know about our services should they ever need them."

"Oh, I see. Well, you can send me your information and I'll look it over."

"Sure, I have you at (address of potential customer), is that right?"

"Yes, that's right"

"Great, I'll get that out to you today. I'd also like to give you our website address if you'd like to check that out. It has lots of information about our business and the services we offer."

"Sure, what is it?"

"Our website is _____"

   "Ok, I've got it."

"Ok, thank you for your time, have a great day."

   "Bye."

"Good bye."

   Click...

(That's it! Onto the next call!)

There, you see? It's not that bad. You probably wouldn't hang up on someone who said that to you. It's polite, and it's not pushy. You're just getting some information out there. It sure helps to have dog-walking or pet-sitting as part of your business name, as the mere mention of dogs or animals in the first sentence tends to alter folks' state of mind instantly. The majority of people aren't nasty anyway, and the few that tend to be are not likely to act this way when dealing with a local hometown business. Second, you really aren't selling anything over the telephone or asking for anything. You're just "getting the word out."

The largest obstacle to most calling campaigns is obtaining a list of good leads and making a *cold sale* (agree to upgrade your long distance, agree to take a trip to see a time-share, etc). Your calling campaign has neither of these obstacles! You will have a very reliable list of leads, free of charge, and you aren't trying to make a cold sale! This is the fastest way to get information out to the most qualified leads as cheaply as possible, bar none. It targets qualified leads and identifies your most likely business prospects fast and efficiently. Those who say yes to you sending them information are very likely to purchase your services. In most cases they are saying yes because they really need a dog walker or they don't like the one they have and haven't gotten around to replacing them yet. Remember, making things happen takes courage and a belief in yourself and your ideas. If you weren't doing this for yourself you might very well be an employee doing the same exact thing for someone else! Do it for yourself!

If you are sure you'll break out in hives if you get near a telephone to make cold calls, then I make the following suggestion. Hire a temp or someone you know to make them for you, using your script. It will cost you money, but at least your business will still find the fastest and best way to the market. The trouble is that this method is impersonal, and the temp may be less than enthusiastic. I'm really not sure this is the best option, but the upside of outsourcing the calling campaign is that it will go on every day until the list is complete, and multiple towns can be covered in a short amount of time.

If a calling campaign isn't going to work for you, or the DNCR is too much trouble, then you can take a deep breath and create a mass mailing campaign targeted directly to dog owners via the list you obtained. Keep in mind that the costs associated with direct mail are much higher than telemarketing. In addition to the costs of printed materials and envelopes, you must also consider postage. Postage fees are determined both by weight and rate (First Class, Standard Mail, etc.). Therefore you should carefully consider what type of materials you would like to mail, and what that will cost in terms of postage.

You may want to consider qualifying for bulk mail rates with the United States Postal Service. It's not simply a matter of going down to the post office with a box loaded with letters and asking for a bulk mail rate (also called Standard Mail). The USPS requires that you have a special mailing permit and to pay an annual mailing fee. You will be required to presort and pay postage prior to delivering your mail to the post office where you hold your permit. There are other requirements in addition to the aforementioned. For more information and a direct link to the USPS Business Mail 101 page, please visit the companion site.

Keep your advertising material brief and describe your services. Basically what you want to do here is provide a short letter introducing yourself, your business, and your services. Also, highlight what sets your business apart from others. You may want to include a "special offer" such as:

▶ *Get 5 walks for the price of 4!*

▶ *Get 10% off the first month of service!*

▶ A sample letter can be found on *The Dog Walker's Companion* (DVD).

Refer pet owners to your website for more information. Consider including a refrigerator magnet or other useful item with your company name and contact info imprinted on it.

Mass mail advertising packages

Although similar to a direct mail campaign, the mass mailing advertisers I have worked with don't target a specific demographic or group (such as dog owners), they mail according to specified regions. Also, you are limited by the media and method by which they do the mailing. The upside is they handle all the printing, addressing, labeling, and postage and you only pay a one-time fee per mailing. I've used this method and haven't really found it to be worthwhile. I used a local coupon mailing company that packages a bunch of coupons inside an envelope and mails them to homes in the region you select. I think most people throw them away without opening them. I've received a few clients from them and I suppose even getting two clients from one mailing becomes worthwhile when the income generated eventually pays off the cost to advertise. However, there are much better ways to spend your advertising dollars in my opinion. The problem with this advertising is that households that do not have dogs will also get your coupons. It's really not targeted enough for your business. The following are examples of coupons I created for inclusion in a coupon mailer:

Craigslist

Craigslist has grown into one of the most used classified advertising websites online. Placing an ad is free and reaches hundreds of people. Many dog walkers and dog care professionals advertise on *Craigslist*. Ads run for a week, and then you have to create a new one. Go to *http://www.craigslist.org*

Door knob hangers

You've probably found these on your front door from time to time. Pizza businesses use them all the time in my neighborhood. They are inexpensive to have printed. Take a stack with you every day and walk a few blocks hanging them on people's doors. I'd recommend doing it on a weekday. When people get home from work they'll see it hanging there. It's a great way to get your business noticed, and in most cases you can do it while you walk your clients' dogs!

Fliers

Remember the days of opening a lemonade stand and pinning up your posters all over the neighborhood? Well, it's time to do it again. However, I wouldn't recommend creating them with crayons and magic markers. You want something eye catching that people can read from a distance and that makes them want to come in for a closer look. Take a look at what I did for my business on the next page.

WANTED!

Someone to walk me during the day when you're at work.

Why not call us? It's what we do!

Newburyport Walks Dogs

We offer a range of services to fit any budget.

Check us out online:

www.nbptwalksdogs.com
dogwalker@nbptwalksdogs.com

(999) 222-0022

You can feel free to use this example for yourselves. It was effective, and I got a lot of calls from these. Once you start building a clientele you may put up fliers or door knob hangers in areas where you are already walking dogs. This lets people know you are working in the area. Advertise that joining a dog walking group lowers the per-walk rate! Pretty soon your clients will be selling your business to their friends and neighbors in an effort to get group walks going for their own pets. It's a win for everyone! Please check with your city or town about any ordinances regarding fliers. The following are places to consider putting up fliers or business cards.

▶ Day care centers

▶ Churches

▶ Hospitals *(Talk with the Public Relations Liaison and provide him with your business information. He can provide your name to people who are in urgent need of pet care due to a sudden injury or illness. Also, doctors and nurses tend to work long hours and are likely to need a service such as this if they have a pet.)*

▶ Local Post Offices

▶ Local travel agencies *(if they still exist)*

▶ Veterinarian offices

▶ Groomers

▶ Pet related stores

▶ Library

▶ Coffee shops

▶ Community bulletin boards

▶ Local fitness center

▶ Bus stations

▶ Train stations

▶ Dry cleaners

Car tagging

T his involves printing up mini advertisements, usually three to a standard sized 8.5" X 11" document. You can keep a stack of these in your car and place them under windshield wiper blades on clear, sunny days. A good place to go is a park & ride, as commuters are often the people who really need a dog walking service. Check to make sure the parking lot has not posted signs forbidding car tagging. Many private parking lots forbid it as a lot of people pull them off their car and toss them on the ground, thus littering. Since the litter has your business name on it, it's not a great way to advertise. I don't really recommend it, but it has its place, especially when you really want to saturate a market with your name and get people thinking and talking about your business. Just be aware that this type of advertising tends to produce more negativity than leads.

Promotional items

Getting your name out there is really important. Imprinted magnets, pens, notepads, hats and apparel, and magnetic signs on your business vehicle are excellent cost effective means for doing this. This is something to think about doing once your business is well established. Don't waste time and money on these things yet. The exception may be the signage on your car, which is a constant source of advertising. The benefit of promotional items is exponential—the more items in circulation, the more benefit your business will derive from them. If you plan on doing a direct mail advertising campaign, get some imprinted magnets made up to include with your advertising materials.

Google & Yahoo

If you don't know what *Google* or *Yahoo* is by now, you're not likely to understand what I am going to say here. I'll assume everyone knows what *Google* is. Once you have your website up and running you should advertise with *Google AdWords*.

▶ *http://adwords.google.com*

It's not hard to set up. What *AdWords* does is allow you to select keywords such as *dog walks, pet sitting, kennel, yourhometown,* etc., which get your advertising directly to people who are interested in what you have to sell. It's target advertising like the world has never known. You need it—get it. *Yahoo* also has a similar advertising method and you can check that out at:

▶ *http://searchmarketing.yahoo.com/as*

Take action

1. Determine how much money you can afford to set aside for advertising. This is your advertising budget.

2. Contact the most popular business telephone directory's ad-sales department and obtain a rate-card. Do this for the second largest directory as well. Negotiate and purchase advertising. Be sure to require approval for your ad. You want to make sure there aren't any misspellings or errors (once it's printed there is nothing you can do but wait another year).

3. Call ahead to your town/city clerk and let them know you'd like to get the listing of licensed dog owners for your town. Get the list as soon as it is ready.

4. Determine whether you are going to do a calling campaign or use direct mail. If you decide on a calling campaign, visit the FTC website and follow the instructions. Cull any numbers that are on the DNCR list. Begin the call or direct mail campaigns. Print the calling script from the DVD (if you have purchased it).

5. Contact your local newspaper and get an advertising rate-card and ask to be assigned an account executive. Negotiate and purchase advertising.

6. Visit *Craigslist* and see how other dog walkers are advertising. Post your ad.

7. If you choose to do bulk mail advertising, check your local phone book for leads or look for the bulk mailing company name on the bulk mail you receive at you home.

8. Contact a printer and get rate-cards for printing fliers, door knob hangers, and business cards. Design and purchase those items you will be using when ready.

9. Go online and do a search for "promotional items." Check out the many online stores devoted to these types of items. You won't believe what you can get. Purchase items when ready.

10. Visit *Google* and *Yahoo* and learn about their advertising options. Consider purchasing keyword advertising once your website is up and running.

STEP 5

Equipment

Chapter Summary

This chapter provides suggestions for equipment and gear to purchase for your business. Much of your equipment needs will depend on region, seasons, and type of services you offer. As far as clothing goes, this is about personal preference and climate more than anything. The following items will be covered:

- ▶ Clothing
- ▶ Flashlights
- ▶ Treat bags
- ▶ Reflective gear and safety equipment
- ▶ Leashes
- ▶ Collars
- ▶ Phone
- ▶ Rain gear
- ▶ Key management
- ▶ Maps, directories, and GPS systems
- ▶ Canine aggression deterrents
- ▶ Spray bottles and water-guns
- ▶ First aid kit
- ▶ Personal protection

Clothing

Wear clothing that is comfortable but looks clean and put-together. You don't want to be walking around in old sweats. Yes, I know, the only people you'll be dealing with on most days have four legs and slobber a lot, but building your business is about image, and you don't want your image to be that of a slob. People take notice! If they see a person who looks and acts professional, they are likely to assume you are a professional dog walker, and thus may ask for your business card! There are a few things, though, you will want to purchase beyond your personal wardrobe.

Small headlamp flashlight

If you plan on walking dogs in conditions of limited visibility or when it's dark, make sure you get a headlamp. Not only will it enable you to see where you're going but it will make you visible to others as well. *REI, EMS, L.L. Bean* and just about any outdoor gear store are sure to have them. LED lights are the best. They are lightweight, have high visibility, and their battery life is excellent. They often have different settings that allow for a flashing light at different intervals, which can be helpful if you simply want to be seen but don't necessarily need the light on to find your way in the dark. The most important part is that your hands are free and the light shines at whatever you are looking at.

Treat bag

These are great for dog professionals. It's basically a small draw-string pouch that you can keep small treats in for rewarding good behavior. It clips onto your waistband or belt, which makes accessing it very easy. It also keeps the crumbs from treats confined to the pouch instead of your pockets. This is a must have! I also suggest using *Charlee Bear* treats. They are low-calorie and look like those oyster crackers you get with a cup of soup at a restaurant. Dogs LOVE them!

Reflective vest

This is self-evident, but make sure you have one in your car for when you are walking in low light conditions. According to analysis of U.S. Department of Transportation data, most accidents involving pedestrians occur between the hours of 3PM and 7PM. Lack of conspicuity is a major contributor. Take precautions, accidents can happen at any time, but be especially careful during these hours! Reflective vests work by reflecting light back *at its source*. The vest will work only if cars have their headlights on. That's why I suggest getting a reflective vest that is also day-glow orange or safety orange so that it has high visibility even in the absence of reflected light or in dusk conditions before cars have headlights on. Check out stores that sell running equipment, they're sure to have them.

Personal safety light

This is a small red light that blinks at intervals or stays on constantly. These can be clipped to the waist. If you walk dogs in the dark, you definitely want one in addition to a headlamp and safety vest. Like the example above, stores that sell running equipment are sure to have them.

Other visibility equipment

There are companies that make gear for dogs, such as reflective leashes, vests, and collars. Again, if you walk dogs in the dark on busy streets, invest in some kind of reflective material for the dogs you walk.

Spare leash

Always have one with you. Sometimes clients forget to leave their dog's leash in its usual spot for you, and you can't go rummaging through their house looking for it. Have your own just in case.

Spare collars

It also helps to have several slip-on "Martingale" collars in various sizes in case the client misplaces the dog collar as well. Martingale collars are flat collars that are made with two loops. The large loop is placed around the dog's neck and adjusted to fit loosely. The leash is then clipped to the D ring on the small loop. When tension is applied (the dog pulls against the leash) it pulls the small loop taut, which makes the large loop constrict slightly, thus making it tighter on the neck. This tightening effect is limited and will not choke the dog if they are adjusted properly. These are great for dogs who like to "back out" of their collars.

No-pull collars (the new breed)

Another variation on the collar is a halter. These come in various designs. The one I like most is the *Halti* collar, as it seems to be the most comfortable for the dog when they aren't pulling. These collars are designed to make the act of pulling on the leash un-pleasant without causing pain or potential injury to the animal. It works by applying the force of the dog's pulling to an area more or less under their chin where the leash clips onto the O-ring. When the dog pulls against the leash, the halter causes the dog's head to turn to the side. So, rather than the old choke chains where your dog would simply gasp, gag, and choke as it hauled you along like an oxen, you have a dog whose purpose is constantly thwarted by the very effort it makes. In essence, the more force the dog applies, the less effective the dog's efforts become. This effectively trains most dogs to realize that pulling doesn't get them what they want, but walking on a loose leash does! If you have a poorly trained dog that pulls like a maniac, consider using a *Halti* collar. Make sure you clear it with the dog's owner first, and even suggest they try using it for themselves. At first the dog will fight it like nobody's business. He will stop, roll on the ground, paw at the halter, and generally make you feel awful for putting it on him. If you hold your ground, the dog will eventually accept it as part of the deal. The dogs I know push their noses into it because they know it means they are going for a walk! These collars come with instructions on how to use them and what to expect when you do. Make sure to read them!

▶ A demonstration can be seen on *The Dog Walker's Companion* (DVD).

Mobile phone

Be sure to put your clients' contact information on your cell phone. Also make sure to have your clients' veterinarian and an emergency animal hospital programmed in. Police, fire, and animal control officer telephone numbers should be programmed as well.

Rain gear (jacket and pants)

You will be expected to walk dogs in all but severe weather. Rainy days aren't justification to cancel your walks. Be sure to have some good rain gear. Water resistant and breathable are ok, but in my area it rains enough that I prefer serious waterproof clothing. I do not recommend using an umbrella, as you'll need your hand free to do other things. I own a rain jacket (with hood) and bib rain pants for when it's really pouring. Having a dry torso and soaked legs isn't my idea of staying dry! You'll want to invest in a comfortable pair of waterproof, insulated shoes as well.

Key ring with key tags

Don't put client names or addresses on their keys. Assign each client a number and number the keys respectively. Numbered keys betray no information to someone should they find the keys on the roadside. Put an "if found" tag on them and write only your cell phone number on it.

▶ *Example: If found please call 999-888-1000*

Once you have a lot of clients, the keys are going to get very confusing. If a client discontinues your service but wants to be able to call on you as needed, take the key off your regular ring and put it on another ring with infrequent clients. You don't want to carry all your keys on one ring. In the event that you lose a ring, all the keys will not be lost.

Keep in mind also that if you lose a client's key, you will have to inform them of the loss. If they decide to purchase new locks, you should offer to pay for them. Some pet insurance companies offer lock protection coverage in the event of lost keys. If you have enough clients you may want to have a "morning" ring and an "afternoon" ring.

▶ Make sure you get two keys from each customer. Keep one key as a backup copy at your home.

Map and business directory or GPS system

You may be spending a good deal of your time in your car, and you never know when something might come up while you are out. I have had to pick up a sick dog and deliver him to a veterinarian, drive a dog to my client's parent's house, etc. Having a map and business directory or a GPS system will come in handy in these circumstances.

Many new cars include a GPS system standard, for others it's still an optional upgrade. You can also purchase them separately. My mobile phone has a software feature built in which offers turn-by-turn directions within the provider's coverage area.

Citronella spray

Canine deterrent spray (for dog aggression). Please see discussion in Step 11.

Spray bottle / spray gun

A small spray bottle filled with water can be a great and harmless deterrent for unwanted behavior such as aggressive barking, especially among puppies and very young dogs. Basically, you spray the water at the dog's face, and it's so surprising and disagreeable to the dog that it interrupts the undesirable behavior. Once you have the dog's attention (we hope), offer a treat to reward them for refocusing attention on you and not barking. The idea here is: barking at other dogs = water in the face; looking at you and not barking = food in the mouth. This won't always work, but it's worth having a spray bottle in your car for those dogs you know have this tendency. The lure of food doesn't hold sway over all dogs, particularly when they are behaving aggressively. The spray bottle is also reasonably effective for shooing away stray dogs.

Pet first aid kit

To purchase a pet first aid kit already stocked with items specifically for pets visit the *American Red Cross* online at *http://www.redcross.org*. A more detailed discussion on pet first aid can be found in Step 8.

Pepper spray

Pepper spray can be carried for personal protection. Check local laws and regulations regarding possession of pepper spray. Some states require permits and/or licenses' to carry it. Be sure to be properly trained in how to use it!

Take action

1. Make an assessment of your wardrobe. Do you have the right kind of clothing? Make a list of the things you need.

2. Consider the other equipment listed in this chapter. Make note of the things you already possess. Plan to purchase the remaining items.

3. Check the resources section of the companion site for links to purchase some of the products I've mentioned here. *http://www.dogzanny.com/resources*

STEP 6

Client Interview

Chapter Summary

T his chapter will prepare you for meeting with clients and conducting successful, productive interviews. The client interview is perhaps the most important part of the process of converting an interested party into a client. This also may be the only face-to-face meeting you ever have with your client, and it's where both you and they decide if it's going to work out. The following items will be covered:

▶ What to bring and why

▶ How to dress for success

▶ Importance of the client interview

▶ Meeting & greeting

▶ Getting safely through the door

▶ How to conduct a client interview

▶ Closing and follow-up

What to bring

When making contact with a potential new customer for the first time, remember to bring the following information and materials:

- ► A smile and good attitude (no, I'm not kidding)
- ► Business cards
- ► Your *welcome packet* (see Step 2)
- ► Service agreement
- ► A pen
- ► A notebook
- ► Plenty of small treats for their dog. Ask for permission from the owner before feeding them!

It seems obvious enough to suggest bringing a smile and a good attitude, but you'd be surprised how many people forget this. A good attitude is contagious, and it makes others feel good about you. Get your attitude up and be happy, you're a dog walker after all!

Your business card will most likely go into a drawer of other business cards and be kept around, while your other material will quickly be lost in piles of papers, the trash, or some file folder somewhere. Make sure you always have a few business cards with you, even when not on duty!

Your attire

few words mentioned here are worthwhile I think. How
should you look going to a client interview? You should
dress appropriately for the work you do. This doesn't mean you
should come wearing clothes covered in dog hair. Wear clothing
that is clean, well matched, in good repair, and is functional. Jeans,
athletic pants, T-shirts (with your logo on them), fleeces, and other outdoor active wear are perfectly appropriate. You should not
come wearing a dress shirt, or in heels and a silk blouse. Even if
you never walk the dogs yourself and hire employees to do this for
you, you should dress as if you do.

The one caveat I make is for very high class dog walking businesses that cater to the very well-to-do. These people are used to
dealing with business owners and not the hired help. In this case,
you probably don't actually walk the dogs yourself, and even if
you do, you should dress business-casual for the initial meeting.

The importance of the client interview

The client interview is where you really sell yourself and your
business. It is where you, your client, and their dog get to
know each other and make sure everyone is comfortable with the
arrangement. The client wants to know they can trust you, and at
the outcome of this meeting you will be able to determine whether
you have that trust. Put the client at ease by being relaxed. Be sure
to make eye contact when you are listening to them speak and
when you are speaking. It is a well known fact that persons that

cannot make eye contact seem untrustworthy, as if they are hiding something. If making eye contact is something you struggle with, start practicing every time you purchase something from a store. Look the clerk in the eye when you bring your items to the counter and when you speak to them.

The other purpose of client interviews is to go over your services, policies, background, and exchange information. You'll want to learn about their pets and what they want for them. You will be able to directly respond to questions and concerns. By learning more about your customers and their pets you will be able to offer them the services they require based on their unique circumstances.

Meet & greet

You arrive at your potential client's doorstep for your initial meeting. Remember to look the owner in the eye and say hello to them FIRST, even if the dog is the first to greet you. They are the person hiring you, and you want to make sure that they feel that you are working for them. Dog walking isn't a people profession per se, but if you don't have an ability to connect with people—the owners—you are probably not likely to be given the chance to connect with their dogs. After shaking hands, turn your attention to the dog, giving him treats (ask if it's ok) and praise as you head inside.

If the dog is showing aggression, give him time to get used to you before going inside. Ask if it is safe to do so. If you feel at all uncomfortable, suggest that the owner take hold of his dog so that you may safely enter the home. If you do not feel safe entering the home, ask the owner to bring the dog outside on a leash so that you may meet him on more neutral ground. Once the dog has become comfortable, you may attempt to enter the home together. Proceed with caution as the dog may become territorial when you attempt to enter the home. This type of display will warrant a frank assessment of the risks of handling such a dog. Be sure to ask the client about the dog's history and behaviors.

Remember, this is a meeting between you and the dog's owner. Make sure you spend at least as much, if not more time looking at the owner as you do at the dog. The owner will want you to acknowledge and enjoy their dog as much as they do, but they don't want to be secondary in importance during this initial interview. After all, it's not the dog that will be writing the checks! I cannot stress this enough.

Getting down to business

I like to start the conversation by asking the owner about their dog and what they are looking for specifically for their dog. Most parents love to talk about their kids, and it's not much different with pet owners and their pets. This gets the ball rolling, and talking about their dog tends to put most people in a relaxed mood. Try to maintain this relaxed mood throughout the interview. If you get "right down to business" you will come off as a sales person, and it could put off even "strictly business" types. After discussing the dog's and the client's needs, explain what services you provide, emphasizing the care, reliability, and any other points about you or your business that set you apart from the competition. Make sure to point out where in your welcome packet they can find the information you are discussing with them. One way I have found to keep the focus off you and keep things on track is to provide owners with a copy of your information packet and go through it with them during the interview. That way you can answer questions as they come up and expand on areas they are interested in. Ask what their dog likes and dislikes, and be sure to find out whether the dog has any habits or behavior that could be dangerous, such as swallowing stones, biting, etc. Take notes, you will be surprised how much you can forget!

Finally, provide owners with the information and contact form to fill out, as well as the service agreement for them to sign. You may fill out your portion ahead of time, sign it, and leave it with them to complete. They can leave the completed materials for you to pick up on the first day of service. Or, you can have them fill them out while you wait. I like to leave the materials as this lowers the sense of pressure. After you present them with the legal agreement—which tends to raise their resistance—turn their attention back to your service. You want to end the interview on a high note.

Let them know that you will provide them with a notebook which you and they can use to maintain contact day-to-day. I know of other dog walking services that leave a daily "report card" as a means of communication. Report cards are time consuming to fill out and to create, not to mention costly. Using the report cards almost obligates you to leave one after every single visit, which is impractical, especially once you've been walking the same dog, day after day, for months. Honestly, after a while there isn't really that much to say, and a report card starts to become a nuisance for both you and your client. A notebook, on the other hand, sends an inherent message that you expect this to be a long relationship (a notebook has a lot of paper in it). Report cards are fine for vacationers and short duration clients, but for long-term regular clients I opt for the notebook. Notes are dated and left when needed.

Closing and follow up

Finally, tell owners you look forward to taking care of their dog and that you enjoyed meeting them. Compliment their dog in whatever way seems appropriate to you. Plan to send them a follow-up email or letter that very same day, thanking them once again for contacting you, and letting them know you're ready to bring their dog into your dog-care schedule. If you don't hear from them within 3 business days, call them to follow up. Persistence pays off. Don't be a nag, but stick with them and let them know you are serious about *your* business by taking *their* business seriously. If they tell you they've found another dog walker, ask them what was the deciding factor. Try to pin them down on what exactly it was. Most people will answer readily when it's a simple issue such as price, schedule, or types of services. If they have trouble articulating an answer, figure it's a personality conflict and leave it at that. If you are getting a lot of rejections based on prices and/or services, you should consider offering a plan that reflects the needs of those who are turning you down. Also, ask yourself if you have adequately explained your services and pricing to your potential customer. Sometimes it is merely unclear advertising copy (text of the advertisement) which is the culprit, not the actual prices or services.

Most of all, relax and have fun, you aren't selling vacuums, you are offering your customer peace of mind and satisfaction knowing their dog will be in good hands and well taken care of. Take pride in this responsibility and enjoy all the benefits that come with spending your days with dogs, out in the fresh air, and getting exercise at the same time!

Although I have made every attempt to provide as much information as I can to ensure that your client interviews are successful, I recognize that seeing how an actual interview is conducted is perhaps the best way to put all the pieces together. If you have not already done so, you may want to consider purchasing *The Dog Walker's Companion* (DVD) and watch the full demonstration client interview.

Take action

1. Practice making eye contact with people. Talking to store clerks, coworkers, family and friends is a good place to start.

2. If you've purchased *The Dog Walker's Companion* (DVD) please watch the demonstration client interview.

3. Complete your welcome packet and put all the materials you will need for your first client interview together so they are ready to go.

4. Rehearse presenting your materials to an imaginary client by yourself a few times and then enlist the help of a friend or family member to act as the client once you're ready.

STEP 7

Walking the Dogs

Chapter Summary

You've been hired, congratulations! Now comes the actual business of dog walking—walking the dogs! In this chapter you will be introduced to some of the issues you will want to consider before actually taking your new four-legged client for a walk. The following items will be covered:

- ▶ Safety for you and the dog
- ▶ The needs of the dog
- ▶ Being efficient
- ▶ Your personal pleasure
- ▶ Encountering thoughtless dog owners
- ▶ Parks and off leash dogs
- ▶ Leash aggression

Safety for you and the dog

Choosing a route has many implications, not least of which is your pleasure and safety. What do you do when a client wants you to take their dog for a walk in a nearby park, but getting to that park involves a death-defying street crossing of four lanes of traffic with no crosswalk? Needless to say I would refuse this request! Only you can determine the level of risk you are comfortable with. The above example may seem extreme, but I assure you, it's not. Clients often have favorite routes which they may want you to take ol' Fido on. If it would make or break the deal, and I could minimize the risks, then I would consider the client's route. In most cases however, clients leave it up to you. In some areas your route options may be quite limited, in others, endless.

Being a Dog Walker requires a certain amount of personal fortitude. You go out in just about any weather and in all seasons. Let's say it is winter and your favorite route involves walking in areas that are rarely plowed and are often icy. I would strongly caution against this route, even if you are wearing traction control devices on your boots. Dogs can be unpredictable, and a dog that pulls you suddenly on ice could land you in the hospital, unable to walk dogs! Your business might survive if you have reliable employees, but why risk injury? In my city it's a law that sidewalks must be cleared after a storm, however this rarely ensures that there will not be any ice. I often have to walk dogs in the street because the sidewalks are too treacherous. If the street is too busy with traffic, perhaps the best bet would be to take the dog out into its own yard or even into your car for a quick trip somewhere safe to take your walk (be sure to include a provision in your service agreement that allows for this possibility).

I relate this because once you have gotten knee deep in the business you may just try to work through dangerous circumstances because the effort involved in minimizing risks entails some kind of inconvenience. When weighing things like inconvenience versus an obvious risk—and it's *your livelihood* on the line—you need to minimize needless risk. These are just some of the areas of risk management you should think about. Others include routes that take you near dangerous dogs, crime prone areas, or remote areas. You should always be cautious about walking at night. Being consistent is great for the dog and his owners, but it can work against you if human predators are aware of your schedule. With this in mind, take whatever lawful precautions are necessary to make yourself safe. Talk to local police if you are unsure of an area or have concern for you or your employees' safety from crime. When in doubt, cancel the service for any client where the risks cannot be managed to your satisfaction.

Needs of the dog

C onsider the health of the dog and/or any physical limitations he may have. For example, steep slopes or stairs would be very difficult, if not impossible, for a dog with hip dysplasia. You will want to choose a route that is comfortable and safe for such a dog.

Probably the most important need is the need to eliminate! If you have been fortunate to know many dogs in your life, then you know that they all develop their little idiosyncrasies, not least of which is where they choose to eliminate. Be sure to ask the client where their dog likes to eliminate, as this is a most crucial piece of information. Some dogs I've known will only eliminate on grass, some on leaves, and others cement. It all depends on what environment they have become accustomed to. With that in mind, choose the route that will offer your furry friend a place to eliminate. Do not allow your dog to eliminate on private lawns, gardens and the like. Try to find spots that are unobtrusive, neglected, or town/city owned. The last thing you need is to be confronted by an angry neighbor for allowing Spot to "spot" his lawn. *Always* be sure to pick up after the dog. Even if it's a tiny amount of impossible-to-pick-up diarrhea, bend over and make the effort to look like you're picking something up. Murphy's Law will have a neighbor peering out their window watching to see if you do. Remember, all the neighbor will have seen is the dog squat, not how much or what came out. If you walk away without picking it up, your client will hear about it and so will you!

Efficiency

T his is another simple concept, and one you would figure out for yourself fairly quickly. Choose a route that offers a loop that, walking at a normal pace, will result in about 5 minutes less than the time allotted for the walk. Use these 5 minutes as a buffer for sniffing time, elimination, a chat with a passerby, or the like; that way by slowing down or hustling a bit you can make sure that the time out does not exceed the service purchased. Is it the end of the earth if you go over by 5 minutes? No, not in the beginning; however, every 5 minutes you go over is time unpaid for, and it can wreak havoc on your schedule. Work on finding a route that will allow you to control the time spent out on the walk.

Personal pleasure

L et's not beat around the bush. You didn't choose to open a manufacturing plant; you've decided to care for animals. With that in mind, dog walking is as much a lifestyle choice as it is a profession. Will you get rich walking dogs? Maybe, if you're interested in expanding and building a large business. Otherwise, you are creating a small business as an alternative to working for someone else, or as supplemental income. With a little effort you will enjoy freedom from offices and cube farms, have more time for yourself and family, get more sleep, and enjoy the benefits of spending your time in the fresh air getting exercise with the best stress relievers on the planet, dogs. Try to find clientele in areas where you want to spend time walking. It's a delicate balance between financial needs and lifestyle, and you'll learn how to strike a balance that works for you.

Encountering thoughtless dog owners

E ven in parks where there is a leash law there are plenty of clueless people who think the whole world belongs to them and allow their silly, but friendly dogs to run loose. Their logic goes something like this: "My dog isn't aggressive; he's just a big love. The leash law is for aggressive dogs, not mine." What they don't think about is what it's like for people who want to take their *shy dog, dog-reactive[1] dog, or fearful dog* for a walk. In a place where all owners obey the law and *all dogs* are on a leash it isn't a problem at all. If you find this utopia, let me know!

More often than not, some dog owner will set their dog loose and it will come running right at you and create a huge scene. These owners usually have zero control of their dogs and they

---

1. A dog-reactive dog is one who behaves either aggressively or excessively toward other dogs (they may simply go berserk but not necessarily in an aggressive way). Aggression doesn't always have to be a part of dog reactivity but it often is. If you are walking a dog-reactive dog, make sure she is on a leash at all times and don't walk her where dogs are allowed off leash, or you're just asking for trouble.

may make some lame attempts to call their dog back, which is really only for show as they don't have the least bit of hope that their dog will listen to them. The fact that they have zero control of their dog can mean a lot of things, but what it usually means is that they were too lazy to properly train their dog, and rather than get yanked along by a dog who has no leash manners, they just turn the dog loose to make *their* walk more enjoyable, completely ignoring the inconvenience it causes others. Can you tell I have some issues here? Yes, I guess I do. It really boils down to consideration for others, and unfortunately many people simply have none.

The lesson here is simple. You aren't going to be like those people. You are a professional who will obey the dog ordinances and laws because not doing so will reflect poorly on your business, and may put your business at significant risk. You know these situations can and will happen, and you now know what to expect. Be aware of your surroundings and take precautions to avoid dog-dog conflicts whenever possible.

Parks, off leash dogs, and leash aggression

L eash aggression is a strange phenomenon. You put a normally mild-mannered dog on a leash and upon seeing another dog; he becomes a ferocious rabid wolverine. Who is to say exactly why this occurs? My theory is that the dog feels vulnerable (he is) and limited in his ability to defend himself (he is). I also feel that some dogs feel *empowered* by being attached to you by a leash. They feel confident that you will be able to rescue them should they actually have to put something more substantive behind their bark (if push comes to shove). I rather think that the accepted term "leash aggression" is misleading. Sure, what we see is more aggression coming from certain dogs when they are on a leash, but the term leash aggression doesn't in any way suggest the reason for it. Is it frustration, anxiety, or over-confidence? The end result is aggression but what's the root cause? Perhaps it would be better defined as leash *reactive* which may *lead to aggression*. When talking about leash aggressive dogs one must be careful not to assume that the reasons for that aggression are the same for all dogs. As is often the case, the leash is provoking something that wouldn't otherwise happen. Be aware of this.

The following is a good example of what you can expect at parks when you are walking a dog-reactive or leash-aggressive dog. Several months ago I was in a park walking a dog and minding my own business, when out of the clear blue another dog appeared (owner was nowhere in sight) and my dog went ballistic (she is leash-aggressive and dog-reactive). My dog was pulling me around like a rag doll and the stray dog stayed just out of reach (especially true when the loose dog is smaller than your dog). So here I was, holding onto my dog (the responsible handler) and the other person (the irresponsible handler) did not even attempt to intervene when she finally did come into sight.

This is a bad situation, and one you will find all too common. It's bad for several reasons. By holding your dog back, you put her at a major disadvantage should it become a fight, and it gives the other dog a false sense of confidence while increasing your dog's anxiety and tension. Many people have found that by dropping the dog's leash before the strange dog approaches, they alleviate this tension and the dogs are free to engage in normal social behaviors, which may reduce conflicts. Sometimes this is the case, but it also carries significant risks (loss of control of your dog and/or a dog fight). In the case I described above, doing so would not be a good idea as the damage of being leash-restricted was already done. My dog had already experienced the frustration of being on the leash. Dropping the leash at that point would simply lead to a direct conflict. I personally do not do this with my clients' dogs as I rarely walk them in areas where off-leash dogs can be found. Never release a dog in your care if you cannot reliably get the dog to come back to you with a verbal cue or if doing so would endanger it, you, other persons, dogs, or animals. I would not recommend releasing a dog-reactive dog or one that might initiate aggression toward the intruding dog(s). Often the most conservative approach is the superlative one. Do your best to get your dog away from the situation. Call the other owner to get their dog.

Unfortunately, I cannot tell you exactly what to do because every situation is unique. As you become more experienced, learn the personality of the dogs you walk, and understand canine body language, you will be able to manage these situations with greater ease or avoid them altogether. Be sure to read Step 11 on dog fights for a further discussion about actions you might take if things get out of hand.

Take action

1. Practice timing your walks with your own dog. Get to a point where you can leave the house and return within the block of time you offer your clients.

2. Practice using a *Halti* collar or *Gentle Leader,* and a *Martingale collar*.

3. Practice dog avoidance techniques; start thinking about what you would do if you were walking a dog-reactive dog.

4. Get all your equipment together and try it out. Get comfortable using things like a treat bag, *Halti* collar, and headlamp.

Step 8

Understanding and Minding the Animals in Your Care

Chapter Summary

This chapter discusses the importance of being knowledgeable and prepared to care for dogs and other animals. As a professional animal care provider it is critical that you learn about dog behavior, training techniques, and caring for sick or injured animals. It is their well being that you have been entrusted with. The following items will be covered:

▶ The importance of, and how to obtain, pet first aid training

▶ How basic obedience training techniques can benefit your business

▶ The importance of understanding how dogs communicate and learn

American Red Cross, Pet First Aid guides and classes

Dog and Cat First Aid Guides with DVDs and a Pet First Aid course have been developed by the *American Red Cross*. They are great resources and well worth the time and money.

Some local *Red Cross* chapters offer classroom-based instruction as well as at-home study options. You will learn to:

▶ Administer medications

▶ Recognize an emergency

▶ Perform CPR and first aid

▶ Treat common problems and emergencies requiring immediate attention

▶ Stock a pet first aid kit

To find out more and to purchase a pet first aid kit already stocked with items specifically for pets, visit the *American Red Cross* online at *http://www.redcross.org*.

Learn basic obedience techniques

Dog owners often fancy themselves knowledgeable about dogs and dog behavior. To some degree anyone who has lived with a dog is an expert in a limited way. Dog owners will be familiar with a select breed and personality unique to their particular dog. Just as with humans, knowing one person very well doesn't make you an expert on human behavior. In fact, dog owners may know little about what their dog is actually saying to them. Many dog owners have never been to a formal obedience class with their dog. If they have, it's most likely a puppy kindergarten class, and often that's about as far as it goes. You are in a unique position to positively affect your client's relationship with their dog through your knowledge of dog behavior and training techniques. Being a dog walker will give you a wide experience of many breeds, circumstances, and personalities to draw from. It is also necessary to learn from others through reading, coursework, and training clubs. Having a solid understanding of how dogs learn and communicate is critical to becoming an accomplished handler and trainer of dogs.

The Dog Walker's Companion (DVD) includes well-tested and easy-to-learn basic obedience training techniques that all professional dog walkers should be well versed in. Topics covered are: sit, down, sit-stay, down-stay, leash manners, and not jumping up on people. Even if you don't plan on adding dog training to your list of services, knowing basic obedience training techniques will be important for the following reasons:

▶ Your clients will feel more comfortable when they see you applying training methods that get results, even just for simple commands like *sit*, *down*, and *stay*.

▶ Your confidence will improve as you begin to communicate more effectively with dogs.

▶ It will improve your relationship with your clients' dogs, and it will improve their relationship with their own dog. A well behaved dog makes for a happy dog and happy owners.

▶ Your appearance when out in public will be that of a professional.

How do dogs think?

Having a toolbox of training techniques is only half of the story. World class dog trainers don't just know techniques—they know behavior as a science. Beyond understanding how dogs *learn*, the study of dog behavior seeks to understand how dogs *think and communicate*. There is much going on in the study of canine cognition these days, and there is a lot of material worth reading. I would suggest starting with, *The Dog Listener,* by Jan Fennell and *The Other End of the Leash,* by Patricia McConnell. Having a good understanding of how dogs think and what makes them tick will help you and your business in many ways; from devising training techniques that cater to the personality and breed of a specific dog, to helping you and your clients understand strange or complex behavioral patterns. Consider taking an animal cognition class if you live near a college or university that offers one. Start taking your dog to an obedience club, or if you don't have your own dog, borrow someone else's! Or even go just to watch.

Take action

1. Visit the *American Red Cross* online or call your local chapter. Enroll in a Pet First Aid course or take it online. *http://www.redcross.org/*

2. If you purchased the DVD companion video, watch the basic obedience videos. Or get a good dog training book that covers sit, down, sit-stay, down-stay, not pulling on leash, and correcting jumping up on people.

3. Practice the obedience techniques on your own dog until you are comfortable with how they work and/or you start getting some results!

4. Read *The Dog Listener* by Jan Fennell and *The Other End of The Leash* by Patricia McConnell.

5. Research what courses your local colleges offer that would be helpful to your business or understanding and training dogs. Consider expanding your search if local schools don't have what you're looking for; many colleges offer online courses as well.

6. Consider getting a trainer certification or working with your own dog to get some obedience titles under your belt.

7. Join a dog training club.

8. Help out at your local animal shelter.

STEP 9

Earning Trust

Chapter Summary

T rust is something you earn, and once lost is very hard to re-
gain. Trust is also a key element in your success as a dog
walker. In this chapter we will go over some behaviors that can either reinforce trust, or erode it. Remember, as the old saying goes:
a good reputation takes a lifetime to build and only a moment to
destroy. The following items will be covered:

- ▶ How consistent service leads to trust and client
  satisfaction
- ▶ How your actions may appear to others and affect their
  perception of you
- ▶ The wacky things clients might do to test you

Be consistent

T ry to show up at the same time every day. Well-meaning
neighbors will often report your activities to owners. The
more consistent you are, the more likely it is that they will recognize you for being a reliable service. The neighbors may in turn
decide to call on you to walk their own dogs some time! Make
sure the duration of the walk is not shorter than the time you

agreed upon in your service agreement. This seems obvious, but some days you may be running behind and could be tempted to shortchange a walk to catch up—this is a mistake. It's better to be a little late to an appointment than to shortchange one.

Incidentally, much the same can be said for earning the trust of your furry friends. Consistency in your actions and training methods are important to dogs because as they learn what to expect from you, they get used to you. This builds their confidence and reinforces a solid relationship. Earning the trust of your canine companions also involves having a genuine interest and enthusiasm in them and playing with them often.

How do your actions appear to an observer?

Always be aware of how your actions would look to someone else. You should never yank or administer leash corrections on a client's dog unless failing to do so would put yourself or another living being in danger. The problem with using corrections is how they will appear to neighbors and friends of the owner's dog. They could easily be mistaken for mishandling. A person administering leash corrections may appear authoritarian, unfriendly, and/or out of control (even if this is not the case).[2] None of these traits are ones you want to have associated with yourself or your business. Not to mention, the dog may develop a fear of you, which

2. Aversive conditioning can be effective and necessary under certain circumstances, however its usefulness is limited and requires a knowledgeable trainer who understands what s/he is doing and can assess a dog's abilities and receptivity to a given training technique. More often, reward based training can effect the same change with little potential for adverse negative effects.

certainly won't be endearing to the owner if he sees his dog cringing or cowering when you come near.

These types of corrections may have their place under certain limited circumstances, but by and large they are often misused and are thus ineffective. If you want to work to correct bad behavior, I suggest reading some training books or taking a dog training class from your local Humane Society. Once you have some knowledge, you should ask the owner if they would mind you working with their dog while on walks to correct certain things like barking, pulling, etc. I wouldn't consider training someone else's dog with anything but *positive reward based training* unless you are a professional trainer and know what you are doing. With positive reward based training, even if your timing is off (timing is everything in training) you probably won't create new problems or exacerbate old ones, as could be the case with *positive punishment* (leash corrections, shakedown, etc.)—where you can amplify existing fears or damage your relationship with the dog. Using a spray bottle to help correct reactive barking is aversive, but really quite mild, and as long as you get the permission of the owner to employ this training technique, you should be fine. If the dog reacts to the bottle with fear or some other exaggerated behavior, I would discontinue using it.

Be ready for anything

Clients will often "test" you, sometimes in very subtle ways. For example, I had a working agreement with one client that allowed for a 20 minute service which could either be yard-play or a walk on the street. Ninety-nine percent of the time I took her dogs for a walk, but one day, because of a personal injury, I decided to let them play in their yard. The next time I was scheduled, the client did not leave my payment as was customary, but had left a note instead asking me why I had not come the prior day. Baffled, I called her from my cell phone and told her I had indeed come the prior day. I asked her why she thought I had not. Her answer: Because she had left the leashes twisted up and hanging from the wall and they were in the same position when she came home from work (in other words, they had not been used). I was stunned. Needless to say, after I explained what happened she was apologetic. I was fortunate that she gave me the opportunity to explain myself; someone else might have just fired me without explanation. Most people aren't this neurotic, but it is understandable that they will attempt to ascertain if their best friend is getting the services they paid for. The best way to set their minds at ease is through consistent service and frequent communication.

STEP 10

Troubles You May Encounter

Chapter Summary

This chapter deals with issues that arise from handling difficult dogs and/or clients. The behavior of both humans and animals is a fascinating subject, and much larger than the scope of this book. That said, we will limit our discussion of behavior (human or animal) to how it impacts your business. The following items will be covered:

Difficult dogs

▶ What constitutes a difficult dog?

▶ Risk assessment

▶ Dog-dog reactivity

▶ Assessing what you can handle, and options for dealing with dog-reactive dogs

Difficult clients

▶ Are they worth the trouble?

▶ The types of difficult clients you may encounter

▶ Trusting your instincts and taking precautions

▶ Structuring your business and practices to eliminate potential problems

Don't let the tone of this chapter discourage you. Most of your dogs and clients will be of the desirable type. It's really a very small number of them that create problems, and I mention them only to warn you so that you are prepared and have some ideas about what to do should you encounter them. The fact is that in the seven years I have been doing this, I have only encountered a very small handful of dogs and people who belong in this chapter. So take heart and realize that this is just information to keep somewhere in case you need it, but it's hardly worth spending a great deal of energy and time worrying about!

Difficult dogs

You may have heard the platitude, "there are no bad dogs." Well, that's a comforting thought, isn't it? Be that as it may, there are dogs that bite and hurt people and other dogs. They may not be "bad" in so much as they are "malevolent," but a bite is a bite if you know what I mean. You can go on and on about how the dog's behavior is the result of upbringing (the environment) while others will argue just as forcefully that it's the genetics (breed). This is the long standing *nature vs. nurture* debate. The bottom line is it really doesn't matter if the dog was born bad or became that way through a bad environment or a combination of both—at the end of the day you have a behaviorally challenged dog and you have to deal with it.

The most important thing for you to determine is if the undesirable behavior is manageable or worth the risks involved. If you aren't a dog trainer, I do not advise trying to modify a behavior you feel is undesirable or for dogs with a history of chronic aggression—especially toward people. Without the proper training, you will in all likelihood make the problem worse and possibly put yourself or others at risk of injury. Not to mention, it would be unethical to apply behavior modification techniques to someone's dog without their consent and without the proper training. So don't imagine that you'll be the great lion tamer!

The first thing you want to know is if the dog is a danger to you or other people. If by questioning the client or through your own experience you find this to be a possibility, <u>drop the client immediately</u>! I'm not kidding. It's just not worth it. The dog may indeed be a wonderful animal (once you get to know her), but the risks you take in handling such an animal, even with insurance, far outweigh the return. Now, if the owner has a secure private yard that will contain the dog, and you feel confident that you are safe from harm, then perhaps you can go ahead and let the dog out into that private yard as your service rather than a public walk. There is probably still some risk there, though minimized. In the end it's your call. <u>Again, I recommend that you NOT accept a dog/ client relationship if the animal is aggressive toward people</u>. Even if the owner assures you that it's harmless, if you knowingly accept a dog who behaves this way, you are accepting responsibility for what might happen, and that may result in a person or animal getting hurt. A good way to let the client down without offending them is by saying, "I'd really love to help you out with your dog but my insurance provider will not cover me for dogs with known aggressive tendencies. I really can't afford the risk, I'm sorry."

A much less worrisome behavioral issue you will likely encounter is dog-dog reactivity. The most common problem encountered on public walks besides leash-pulling is dog reactivity toward other dogs. What this basically means is that they may bark at, lunge at, act overly exuberant towards, bully, threaten or attack other dogs. Dogs that are reactive toward other dogs are a nuisance, but hardly uncommon. Most dogs display at least some reactivity to other dogs. In fact some dogs are breed selective (they like certain breeds and dislike others). Alas, dogs didn't get the memo about political correctness! My editor mentioned to me that her Lab *loves* to play with other labs. Together with another enthusiastic lab they can create as much mayhem as two antagonistically aggressive dogs, albeit with a good deal less danger!

I have noticed the propensity for reactivity is greater in some breeds than in others, just as some breeds are more likely to herd than others (I've never seen a Husky in a herding competition). Terriers for example can be quite reactive, while many Golden Retrievers and Labradors tend to rank quite low on the reactivity scale. However, all dogs have the potential to be either reactive or non-reactive. Chances are you will have at least a few reactive dogs in your clientele. The important question is, how reactive are they, and will I be able to handle and maintain control of them under any circumstances? It's critical that you make an honest self-assessment here. If you are satisfied that you can handle a 170 lb. Mastiff that is lunging and barking across the street at another dog while you're standing on an icy sidewalk, then go for it! Can you hear my sarcasm? If you think you can handle this dog in all cases *except* icy conditions, perhaps you can work something out with the client so that in icy conditions you can instead let him out for some yard-play.

Get creative—reactive dogs need exercise too! It's up to you to figure out how you can provide a service while protecting your business and your person. I would say at least 50% of all the dogs I've walked are dog-reactive in some circumstances, even if they have been properly socialized. I walk several dogs that regularly attend doggy daycare and yet are still reactive to strange dogs we pass on the street. It's a fact of dog walking. You have to decide what you can handle and accept only those dogs that fall within your parameters. Step 11 discusses ways of dealing with dog-dog aggression.

Difficult clients

What is probably more troubling than a difficult dog is a difficult client. You may have been told that, as a business owner, you must accept and deal with difficult clients as a cost of doing business. Is this true? Yes—sometimes. However, time has an equal relationship to money. How much time you spend on dealing with difficult clients should be determined and weighed against the amount of money they bring into the business. All the money in the world does you very little good if you don't have enough time to enjoy it. In a dog walking business, a difficult client is rarely worth the money. In other types of businesses one client can represent a huge amount of revenue, but for dog walking, this rarely is the case.

In the beginning, as you begin to carve out your market share, you will inevitably pick up the rejects from other dog walkers. These are the clients whom other dog walking services deemed were not worth the trouble. You may choose to bite your tongue and deal with them as you develop a customer base, then part ways down the road if they are still a pain in the rear.

Another group of undesirable clientele can be disagreeable people by nature who are often mistrustful of everyone. You will know this type of client because they will be calling you fresh from firing their last dog walker. You may even find that they've gone through several dog walkers before finding you. Their story is always the same. "The last dog walker didn't do this or that…" If past behavior is an indicator of future actions, then you already know where this relationship is going. I would say fully 90% of these types of clients will wind up finding some reason to let you go within 12 months, but that's enough time for you to develop a base of reliable clientele.

Much like society at large, there are a small percentage of people who may call you that are downright scary, and I would run, not walk away from them. Trust your gut instincts, even if there is nothing obviously wrong. If you have that "feeling" that something isn't right, LISTEN to it and get out of the situation! Make up an excuse and leave immediately. You might even think of some canned excuses beforehand so you'll be ready. Also, be sure to let someone else know if you will be visiting a new client. Provide your friend with the name, address and telephone number of the potential client. Let your friend know that you will call after the appointment, and if you don't call within a certain amount of time, she should call you on your cell phone. If she can't get in touch with you within an allotted timeframe, she can get involved by calling the police.

Avoid clients who tell you they are in the process of suing anyone they have hired to do work for them, such as carpenters, house cleaners, asphalt installers, a mechanic, a past dog walker, or veterinarian. You don't want to be on that list do you? Another kind of scary client is one that has more on his/her mind than dog walking. I think you know what I mean here, and this goes for male dog walkers as much as female. There is a long, long list of risks here that I'm sure an adult can well imagine, and I suggest having nothing to do with these people, even if you do need the business.

Finally, you get the clients who will constantly ask you to do things that are outside the scope of your service. Nickel-and-dimers, they are always trying to get something for nothing. These people just won't stop. I think they must feel resentful that they have to hire you, or that you get to be a dog walker and they don't. They are determined to punish you. These clients can turn into the lawsuit types as well, so beware! They usually don't ask you to do something in a way that gives you the opportunity to say no— they just leave you a note thanking you for doing something that you haven't actually done yet, such as watering the plants. Forget direct confrontation, it's like throwing gasoline on a fire.

I have two suggestions. One is to have a provision in your pet sitting contract for à la carte services and spell out as many of them as you can, assigning each a fair and equitable fee. Provide this to all your customers and in all likelihood the nickel-and-dimers will no longer be an issue. If they ask you to do things outside the scope of the service they purchased, you'll be happy to accommodate them—for a fee! If adding services is not what you want to do, then I suggest sending them a form letter explaining that you will, "no longer be performing tasks that are outside our defined services in order to prevent scheduling delays and to provide a better quality of service to everyone." It will have the appearance of going out to all your clients. This is so they don't necessarily feel that you are singling them out, which could damage your relationship. Keep in mind, these types of people have a tendency to ignore notices like these, assuming they are for "someone else" and couldn't possibly be intended for *them!* At this point you can either accept this aggravation or let them go. If you decide to let them go, cite scheduling problems as the reason.

Every business has its "difficult" clientele. It's easy for a boss to tell an employee to accept the abuse; all he sees is the money, not the humiliation and frustration his employee must endure. Now that you are the boss as well as the employee, things will be different, right? The client's business will affect the bottom line, and now you must decide how much that business is worth. At least the decision is yours and benefits you! Having an understanding of these issues beforehand will give you the edge to head off potential problems and create a stress-free and enjoyable business. Taking care of animals is one of the most rewarding things you may ever do.

STEP 11

Dog Fights

Chapter Summary

This chapter discusses some of the most common reasons why aggression occurs, what can be done to prevent situations from escalating to an actual dog fight, and what you might do if it does. The following items will be covered:

- ▶ The causes of dog aggression
- ▶ The importance of being proactive and taking precautionary actions
- ▶ Warning signs of impending aggression or attack
- ▶ Avoiding and/or minimizing the potential for dog-dog aggression
- ▶ What to do if a fight occurs
- ▶ What to do when the fight is over

Before we get started...

I am offering this chapter on dog fights for information only. I do not suggest you follow this advice without satisfying yourself of it's validity through your own research. I had a lot of consternation about adding this chapter, but I am including it because I think you should be introduced to the fact that dog fights can and do happen. Sometimes, what can *appear* to be aggression to the uninitiated is merely normal dog behavior or even in some cases, play, and should be recognized as such. An attempt to sort out who is in charge or the strongest does not always lead to an actual fight. In many of these situations one of the dogs will back down and a fight will not escalate to involve serious injury. This *backing down* is a necessary behavioral pattern that actually prevents potential disagreements from going too far. Keep this in mind as you go through the chapter and consider your own experiences with dogs. This is a starting point. Your confidence will grow as you become more experienced and better educated.

The causes of dog aggression

There are a great many reasons why aggression occurs. A key reason for dog-dog aggression is lack of socialization (interaction with other dogs). However, proper socialization does not guarantee that a dog will not become aggressive toward other dogs or people. My wife and I put our own dog through two puppy kindergartens, three training classes including the AKC's Canine Good Citizen test, and countless trips to the park to play with other dogs. Yet his disposition toward other dogs remained poor despite our combined experience and efforts to address this proactively. Some common causes of aggression include:

▶ Possessiveness (resource guarding, such as a ball or food dish)

▶ Territory (aggression only in certain locations such as the dog's own car, home, or yard)

▶ Fear (of humans, thunderstorms, prior dog attacks, etc.)

▶ Frustration (being prevented from engaging in normal social behavior by being consistently fenced, leashed, or kept indoors)

▶ Pain or illness (the dog reacts to feelings of pain with aggression)

When observing dog behavior, be wary of the tendency to anthropomorphize dogs. We are looking at the society of dogs[3], not humans, and what dogs think is really anyone's guess. No one can be sure how dogs perceive things, so our words to describe what *we* observe—one dog proving his/her superior strength to another by physical force as *dominance*; another dog rolling over on his/her back as *submission*—may be accurate or inaccurate. No one really knows. You should try not to get emotional about what you see and describe. Try to keep your feelings, history, and issues out of your assessment of the situation at hand, and be as objective as possible. You need to be ready to quickly carry out the most effective solution without hesitation; this requires an objective analysis of the situation, and if it is dominance, fear, or aggression, learn how to safely handle each for what it is.

What I have observed is that the display of aggression is very common when strange dogs meet, especially when on leashes, and even more so when only one dog is on the leash and the other is not (which adds leash anxiety to the mix). Knowing some of the causes of aggression can help you to avoid it, which brings us to the next section.

---

3   I suggest reading the works of L. David Mech. His research into wolf pack social behavior may give us some *clues* about dog social behavior, but remember dogs are not wolves!

Prevention

Practice prevention to avoid getting into situations that can lead to dog-dog aggression. In all my years as a professional dog walker and as a dog owner, I have never had to break up a serious dog fight. One of the reasons for this is that I practice a healthy amount of caution and avoid situations that can lead to conflict. As the old saying goes, an ounce of prevention is worth a pound of cure. Once you get some experience, you will unconsciously find yourself taking precautionary measures to minimize this potential. Aggression is probably the most studied topic in dog behavior. In fact, entire books have been written on this subject alone. I recommend the following books to educate yourself on dog-dog aggression and dog aggression in general:

▶ *Aggression In Dogs: Practical Management, Prevention & Behavior Modification,* by Brenda Aloff

▶ *Feisty Fido,* by Patricia McConnell and Karen London

The first is a huge text that is filled with information and strategies for dealing with many types of aggression. The later is a booklet that introduces the reader to some types of typical aggression that occur when walking dogs on leash and methods for addressing those behaviors.

Please understand it is more effective to know how to prevent a situation or behavior that leads to conflict, than how to stop it once it starts. Learn to read canine body language and avoid potential situations that can lead to conflict! Direct and lasting eye contact between dogs is a huge warning sign that things are going to go south in a hurry. Raised tails, sniffing, and raised hackles are red flags for impending aggression. Distraction is the key. Try to get your dog's attention in order to break the eye contact with the other dog. Move away from the situation if you can. Remember, parks and open spaces are where dogs are sure to be off-leash and are where problems can become unmanageable. If you aren't sure of yourself or the dog(s) you're walking, I would avoid such areas. If you know you are walking a very dog-reactive pooch, go ahead and cross the street or take another route if there is a dog in your path.

Them's fightin' words

No matter how many precautions you may take there is always a chance a dog fight can happen. Any dog fight is a serious event and should not be taken lightly. Injuries can be serious and life threatening. There are many opinions on how to deal with dog fights, some of which I mention below. I strongly encourage you to read the suggested texts and make yourself aware of the options, risks, and techniques available to you.

Citronella sprays that are designed for dog aggression are worth considering. They are designed to be sprayed in the face of the aggressive dog to deter an attack (not necessarily stop one that has already begun). Therefore, they are not a perfect solution, and may not work in all circumstances. Disposable air horns (the kind boaters carry) can also work pretty well to repel an aggressive dog. The principal behind both of these methods is to create a distraction through the introduction of an abrupt and unpleasant stimulus (the spray or the horn). There is also an interesting technique involving the use of an umbrella. No, it's not singing in the rain! This technique is somewhat complex and can be found in Aloff's *Aggression In Dogs*.

Spraying dogs with a hose can work, and I've heard that a dry chemical fire extinguisher that uses *sodium bicarbonate* (a.k.a. baking soda—do not use other types) as its fire suppression agent works very well, but few of us can carry these around with us! Fortunately, citronella spray is not subject to legal restrictions like pepper spray. As far as I know, you don't need a permit to carry a citronella spray, but in many states pepper spray requires a permit. Pepper spray is considered by some to be more effective, but risks of injury to self and dogs are also increased.

There are other ways of breaking up fights that involve two people who know exactly what they are doing and act decisively, but this is not going to be the case while you are out walking dogs and meeting strangers and simple dog-owners. However, if you are starting a doggy day-care I recommend researching and employing techniques to safely and effectively break up dog fights. These other methods involve techniques that are well beyond the scope of this book.

Please understand that you are going to be taking care of dogs every day, and this puts your chances of being witness to a dog fight much higher than your average dog owner. It is your responsibility to protect yourself and your client's dog, in that order. Do not attempt to break up a dog fight if doing so will endanger you or another person. Understand the dogs will be in "fight mode," and won't even know it's you they are biting. Dog bites are VERY SERIOUS!

Do not get into a confrontation with the other dog's owner. If the other owner insists on creating a scene, call the police immediately and explain to them what happened and/or is happening. Make sure you report ANY dog fight to your client immediately. If there are any injuries, you MUST file a report with the local animal control officer or Police. If your dog was attacked by a stray, call Animal Control immediately.

Take action

1. Learn about dog aggression so that you are confident and able to act quickly, either to prevent or address it, should it occur. The books mentioned in this chapter contain a lot of information regarding dog aggression, behavior modification, and techniques to break up dog fights, should they be unavoidable. I strongly suggest reading them before starting your business or attempting to intervene in a dog fight.

2. Once you've done some reading, head to a dog park and observe dog social behavior and body language for yourself. See if you can ascertain what the dogs are saying to each other. Watch for aggression signals; try to identify them.

3. Visit your local shelter and volunteer to work with their dogs so that you may gain some experience. Not only will this work make you feel good inside, it also says a lot about your commitment to dogs and their welfare when it comes time to promote your business.

4. Consider purchasing a citronella spray and learning how to use it.

5. Read *Wolves*, by L. David Mech. It's fascinating stuff!

6. Make sure you have the Animal Control officer and police non-emergency number programmed into your cell phone.

STEP 12

Keeping in Touch

Chapter Summary

This chapter describes how blogging can take your business to the next level and provide a tangible service your clients will love. You will learn what a blog is and how this technology can be used effectively by your business. You will be introduced to options and resources for starting a blog quickly and for little or no money. Be sure to check out the companion site *http://www.dogzanny.com* for additional information and direct access to some of the services mentioned in this chapter. The following items will be covered:

► What is blogging?

► Why blogging is important to your business

► How blogging can be used to enhance your business

► How to start your own blog

► Posting to your blog

► Photos and multimedia

► Earning extra income through advertising

What is blogging?

You have probably heard of blogging, you may even have a blog. For the dilettante, blogging is a form of online journaling that has evolved into a social scene of epic proportions. The name of the game in the "Blogosphere" is to get as much renown as you can get, and as your readership grows, so does the revenue you will receive from third party advertising. Some Bloggers, as they are known, can make a decent living just by blogging. As a result, a whole industry has sprung up to support the blogging community. Internet businesses like *Digg*, *Technorati*, and *StumbleUpon* rank articles and/or sites based on a complex set of rules that correlate to the amount of interest they generate. They do this through user reviews, votes by other readers, and the number of links to the article or site in question. Links to a blog by high profile websites such as news organizations carry more "weight" than links from unknown sites. Those blogs or websites with the highest traffic, user rating, and other sites that link to it rise to the top and have "authority." What started out as online journaling has become an internet subculture of opinions, personal histories, journals, diatribes, and various how-to's written by everyone from twelve year olds to Fortune 500 CEOs.

Why does it matter?

Blogging relates to your business in a most beautiful and beneficial way. Dog walking involves very little human contact. You are the unseen servant who comes and goes while your employers are elsewhere. This can create a sense of distance and isolation from the very people whom you serve. Every once in a while as I enter someone's home to take their dog out, I am suddenly jolted into the realization that I am entering their personal sanctuary and I am taking care of their most beloved friend. This isn't to be understated. You are being given a profound responsibility, even if most of the time neither you, nor the client realizes it. Blogging is a fantastic way to keep it personal and keep a sense of contact with your clients. Sure, it takes a little more time, but it is worth it in my opinion. Here are some ways blogging can benefit and enhance your business:

▶ Facilitate customer involvement and strengthen relationships

▶ Post business news and updates (adding new services, etc.)

▶ Post dog-related news, tips, and information

▶ Post interesting notes about your activities during the day and what your clients' dogs were up to

▶ Post pictures from your walks and outings (This can be done directly from your cell phone.)

▶ Get direct feedback from clients (comments on your posts)

▶ Earn advertising dollars

▶ Maintain communication with clients who are vacationing or working abroad

How do I start?

S etting up a blog isn't that hard. There are a lot of turn-key blogging options available. The two I like the most are:

► *WordPress, http://wordpress.com/signup*

► *Blogger, http://www.blogger.com*

There you can create your free blog in less than 10 minutes and begin posting immediately. The trade-off for the quick-and-easy (and free) is lack of versatility and customized design, and the inability to host your own website. But if you are technically challenged, this is probably your best bet.

For the more adventurous or those with some cash on hand to pay someone else to set up a more professional blog, I recommend setting up the blog on the same Internet address as your business. For example: *www.mydogwalkingbusiness.com/blog*. The best software for creating fantastic looking blogs on your own website is, in my opinion, *WordPress*. You can install this blogging software on your own website. (This is different from doing the signup at *http://wordpress.com/signup*.) It's free and there are tons and tons of templates created by some very talented people that are absolutely fantastic and professionally designed. With *Word-Press*, your options are unlimited. Check out *http://www.dogzanny.com/blog* for a sample blog.

I started out with Blogger, but within a week I migrated over to *WordPress* and set it up on my own web-space. Many hosting companies offer a free installation of *WordPress* onto your web-space. Even if they don't, you can still download and install

Wordpress yourself. If this sounds scary to you, I strongly suggest hiring a professional to set this up for you. I have found *Craigslist* to be a great resource for finding freelance professionals such as web designers. Be sure to check their references and experience (résumé).

It shouldn't take a professional more than 1-2 hours to set up *WordPress.* The people who set up your website should be able to do it. Have them install *WordPress* and set you up with your administrator login at the same time they set up your website and email addresses. That way it's all part of the package.

Managing your own blog with *WordPress* isn't difficult, but if you really don't like computers or technology, it's probably not the option for you. Don't think for a second that if you don't have a blog you won't do well in this business. The blog is a great value added service, but it is certainly not necessary. If it's not something you want to get involved with, consider a monthly email newsletter instead, or just keep in touch with an occasional phone call to your clients. Certain clients may prefer a more traditional method of communication, as they may be technically challenged too!

Informational posts

With a blog, you can keep in touch with your clients as much as you want without having to send messages to each of them individually. Let's examine a case study to help you understand what you can do:

Janet started a dog walking business six months ago. She now has over 20 clients. When she was starting out, she informed her new clients that over the next few months she would phase in a weekly blog to keep in touch with everyone. Now, six months later, her blog is up and running and she is posting messages every other day. Her clients have come to love visiting her blog while at work during the day to see what's new and see a picture of their dog out having a good time! Her clients get to take pleasure in the service they are purchasing for their dog by seeing and hearing about their dog's adventures from week-to-week. Here is a sample post from Janet's blog:

April 14th 2008

Hello Everyone,

Spring has come and the snow has finally melted. That means plenty of wonderful smells are being uncovered for the first time in months. Noses were pressed firmly to the ground on all my walks today. At the park, Bea was the only one interested in chasing the ball!

<Insert photo of Bea chasing a ball>

p.s. I'm reading a great new book on training! I'll post my review when I'm finished.

A blog doesn't have to be complicated. It can be as verbose or as brief as you want. You can include weekly tips, ideas, and other information that you find worth sharing. Your clients can also post comments or responses to the posts you make, just like a message board. You can set your clients up with their own accounts, allowing them the privilege to post comments, or you can set it up to allow posts from anyone (not recommended). It's up to you. You may find that your blog becomes a hotbed of conversation, and who knows; maybe your clients will become friends and meet each other on weekends to let their dogs play together. Either way, it's you and your business that brought this about, and those good feelings will translate to more business, more referrals, and a better quality of life for everyone!

Pictures are worth a thousand words

Taking pictures with a digital camera is a great way to get high quality images onto your blog when you get home, but there is also another great way of keeping the blog updated without a lot of fuss. If you have a cell phone with a digital camera, you can take snapshots while out on walks and use the instant message feature of your cell phone to send the picture to a special email address linked to your blog. Whatever message you send to that email address will appear as a post to your blog immediately! Both *Blogger* and *WordPress* have this feature. Think about the possibilities for keeping in contact! Your clients will be stopping by your blog often to see the picture updates. This also brings visitors to your site because your clients will want to show their friends, and pretty soon you might just have a loyal following of people interested in what you have to say! Welcome to the world of blogging.

Extra income

Another benefit of your blog is that it can earn you money through third party advertising. You can set up an account with *Google* to advertise on your site. The advertising is linked to the content of your site, so the ads will be related to dogs and pets. Every time someone on your site clicks on one of the *Google* ads you earn money! It's passive income. Check out *http://www. google.com/adsense* for more information.

Take action

1. To see a sample blog visit *http://www.dogzanny.com/blog*. There you can get an idea of what you might do with your own blog.

2. Visit *Blogger* and *WordPress* and learn what each has to offer. Create a free blog on each and see which one you like better. Even if you plan on doing one on your own site later, this will give you a good idea of what to expect.

    ▶ *http://www.blogger.com/*

    ▶ *http://wordpress.org/*

3. If you are having your website set up by a professional, make sure they install *WordPress* and set it up for you. You or your designer should choose a theme for your blog that blends well with your website.

4. Once you have your blog set up, visit *Digg*, *Technorati*, and *StumbleUpon* and create an account with each of them. Add your site and blog to their listings. Using these services gets your blog and site into *Google's* search results much faster.

   ▶ *http://digg.com/*

   ▶ *http://technorati.com/*

   ▶ *http://stumbleupon.com/*

5. Start thinking about the kind of information and news you can post to your blog on a weekly basis. Make a list of topics that interest you and would interest your clientele. Stay away from sensitive subject matter that could be off-putting to some people. Don't assume everyone thinks like you do!

6. Check out *http://www.dogzanny.com* for resources and services mentioned in this chapter.

7. Check out *Google AdSense*. Set up an account and install it on your blog, or have your web designer do it for you. *http://www.google.com/adsense*

End Note

Well, we've gone through a lot of information in a short amount of time. This book, *The Dog Walker's Companion* (DVD), and the resources at *www.dogzanny.com* will give you a huge head-start creating and running your own lucrative and enjoyable business. By reading the chapters, acting on the "Action items" at the end of the chapters, and following up with the online resources, you should be ready to hit the ground running when you're ready to start your business.

The future looks bright, folks. I'm so excited for you! I remember when I was just starting my business and how pumped up I was about it. Once you get up and running, get some experience with dogs, and start doing some advanced training with your own dog, you may want to think about the next step: adding dog training services to your dog walking business!

Dog training is a very natural progression for dog walkers. Much more so I think than pet sitters. Dog walkers must have much more control and knowledge of dog behavior than a pet sitter whose job is to care for dogs within a controlled environment (their home or someone else's). Dog walkers learn through experience. They get a huge variety of experience through handling many types of dogs, breeds, and circumstances throughout their career. Experience is critical in training and working with dogs. The wider that experience, the better the potential for the trainer to be successful in his/her training abilities. Read the books I recommend on the companion site. Learn as much as you can and begin to watch for behaviors in the dogs you care for. As you increase your knowledge and awareness, your confidence will grow!

Dog walking is a great way to make money and create a relaxed and flexible lifestyle. Remember to think positively about your life and future. Visualize the outcome that you desire and keep an image of that in your mind as you create and run your business. Don't let a naysayer dissuade you from pursuing your dreams. Try to spend time with positive people who are encouraging to you and have dreams of their own that they are pursuing. The energy of positive thinking is contagious—you'll feel good and move forward.

I've given you a lot of ideas, many of which I have personally used. I'd love to hear your success stories and any ideas you have for improving the business of dog walking or this book. Feel free to drop me a line at *comments@dogzanny.com*. Good luck, and happy trails to you and all your furry friends!

J.D. Antell

References

The Bark, The Dog Culture Magazine. 2008. Media Kit. Online. Available: *http://www.thebark.com/us/pdf_files/bark_media_kit_08.pdf*

IRS. 2008. Home Office Deduction. Online. Available: *http://www.irs.gov/newsroom/article/0,,id=108138,00.html*

Federal Trade Commission. 2008. Do Not Call Registry. Online. Available: *http://www.donotcall.gov*

American Red Cross. Pet First Aid. 2008. Online. Available: *http://www.redcross.org/services/hss/courses/pets.html.* Content used with permission. Courtesy of the American National Red Cross. All rights reserved in all countries.

Aloff, Brenda. 2002. *Aggression In Dogs: Practical Management, Prevention & Behavior Modification*, Wenatchee: Dogwise.

U.S. Department of Transportation, Federal Highway Administration. No date. Pedestrian and Bicycle Safety. Online. Available: *http://www.tfhrc.gov/safety/pedbike/pubs/03042/part1.htm*

Index

A

accidents 73
accountant 13, 26, 38–41
accounting 38, 41
adult dogs 17
advertising 2, 7, 29, 32, 35–40, 46, 47, 53–57, 62–64, 67–70, 85, 123–125,
    130
aggression 43, 71, 77, 82, 87, 92–94, 108, 111, 115–121
aggressive 77, 91, 93, 109–110, 116, 119
Aloff, Brenda 118
Animal Control 121–122
animal shelter 33, 101
anthropomorphize 117
attack 110, 115, 119
attorney 28, 43
aversive 105
aversive conditioning 104

B

barking 77–78, 105, 110
Bark Magazine, The 48
behavior 72, 77, 84, 97–100, 105–109, 112, 116–118, 121, 133
Better Business Bureau 27, 29, 34, 42
bite 108, 111
Blogger 126, 129–130
blogging 15, 47, 49–50, 123–131
bonding 30
brick and mortar 46
business cards 35, 42, 66, 70, 80
business license 29, 42

C

calling script 59
car tagging 53, 67
case studies 12, 20
case study 21–22
cat 16
Certified Public Accountant 13

citronella spray 119–120
client interview 9, 79, 81, 86
clip art 32
cold sale 60
competition 1, 11, 18, 22, 26, 83, 110
confidence 93, 99, 104, 116, 134
consistency 104
corrections 104–105
coupons 35, 42, 63
CPA 13, 26
Craigslist 49, 53, 64, 69, 127
credibility 30, 33, 46, 47
crime 30, 89
customer agreement 35
customer service 11–16, 26

D

Dale Carnegie 16, 26
danger 104, 109–110
deduction 36–39, 42
demographic 6, 48, 62
Digg 124, 131
digital camera 129
direct marketing 53, 57
discussion forums 46
distraction 119
Dog Boot Camp 17
dog fights 17, 94, 115, 118–121
dog parks 18
dog-reactive 91, 93–95, 107–109, 111, 119
dog-related businesses 36
Dog Safaris 16–18, 23–25
dog training 9, 99–101, 105, 133
Dog Walker's Companion, The 9, 31–32, 62, 75, 86, 99, 133
Do Not Call Registry 58, 135

E

education 33
email 15, 48, 54, 85, 127, 129
equipment 38, 71–74, 78, 95

possessiveness 116
prep time 21
professional memberships 27, 29
promotional items 53, 67
puppy 8, 17, 48, 98, 116

R

rain 76, 120
rates 34, 35, 51, 62
record keeping 39
Red Cross 34, 55, 78, 97–100, 135
reward-based training 9
risk vi, 44, 55, 88–89, 92, 109
risks 43–44, 83, 88–89, 94, 108–109, 113, 119–120
RSS 47, 50

S

safety 87, 135
schedule 8, 24, 85, 89–90
service agreement 27, 31, 42, 84, 88, 104
service area 21–22, 51
sick 17, 43, 77, 97
Skinner, B.F. 4
socialization 17, 116
State Parks 18
StumbleUpon 124, 131
suburban 24
synchronicity 6

T

taxes 12–13, 26, 37–39
Technorati 124, 131
telephone directory 53, 69
territory 116
thoughtless dog owners 87, 91
training program 15, 18, 92
trust 15, 28–29, 81, 103–104

U

United States Postal Service 62
urban 21, 24
U.S. Department of Transportation 73, 135

CPSIA information can be obtained at www.ICGtesting.com
Printed in the USA
LVOW10s0131171015

458686LV00028B/319/P